ERLEND BAKKE & STEVE SHOULDER

90 DAYS
TO PROFIT

A PROVEN SYSTEM
TO TRANSFORM
YOUR BUSINESS

Erlend Bakke Publishing

First published in April 2017 by Erlend Bakke & Steve Shoulder

Book design by Access Ideas, access.ideas@yahoo.com
Graphics by Erlend Bakke & James Amora

WHAT YOU WILL LEARN:

Improved Output

Increased Margins

Higher EBITDA

Improved Turnover

Reduced Waste

Decreased Cost Base

7 STEPS TO PROFIT CLIENTS:

TESTIMONIALS

"Steve has made a positive impact on our business. He has technical and people skills which would be an asset to any business that values people with personal drive and the ability to make things happen."

~ Dr Herbert Diess
Managing Director BMW UK Plant Oxford

"Steve is a hugely talented and practical individual who is not happy until he gets the place buzzing. He will always make an impact wherever he goes"

~ Andrew Moore
MBI Business Unit Manager ABB Eutech

"Steve took over the business at a very turbulent time and under intense circumstances and managed it until a successful outcome was achieved."

~ Robert Audas
Group CEO Europackaging

TABLE OF CONTENTS

PRAISE FOR
90 DAYS TO PROFIT

"Insightful and engaging. From business turn around to personal turnaround, It's all here. Whether you are a wanting to become a consultant, are a consultant, a CEO or business owner, this book will change your approach once and for all."

- Brian Smith
UGG Australia Founder

"I have placed Steve into many client companies since 2001 and he has always delivered in spades. Clients, starting with BMW Mini, have always been delighted with the results that Steve has produced. He is one of the top handful of business transformation professionals in the UK and his results speak for themselves. The process that he describes so well in his new book "90 Days to Profit" are elegant in their simplicity and proven value. Any business owner, senior manager or business consultant will benefit greatly from his teachings."

- Norrie Johnston
Founder & Chairman,
Norrie Johnston Recruitment Ltd

"It's simple. If you want more profit in your business, then read this book."

- Mike Michalowicz
Author of Profit First &
Serial Entrepreneur

"There is no point in having a business if there is little or no profit. This book will potentially solve that problem for millions of business owners!"

- Mark Wright
Winner of the Apprentice UK &
CEO of Climb Online

"I quite often call Steve "Oh Great One" when we have our regular catch up calls. He gets a little embarrassed by this but I genuinely hold him in the highest esteem. I am a Kaizen practitioner with some excellent results over the last 30 years and Steve will often call me into a business when he needs someone with my skill set. He is able to galvanise management teams and get everyone in the business behind a common objective far quicker than anyone I know. "90 Days to Profit" is the book that he has written about his methods to transform businesses in the shortest possible time and it is right out of the top drawer. In my humble opinion it should be compulsory reading for every business studies course in the world."

- Ken Padgett
Kaizen Guru and
former Supplier Development Manager - Nissan UK

"Realistic and actionable steps for business owners and consultants everywhere."

- Deri Llewellyn-Davies
"The Strategy Man", Business Growth International

"I have watched Steve applying the principles of the 7 Steps on a daily basis and I can vouch for how effective and powerful it is in practice. The Tesla references are clear to see in his new book and Elon Musk could do a lot worse than buy a copy for every one of his senior managers so that they can apply this process in their business. It might just take them to where they need to be.

- Andrew Hodgson OBE,
Chief Executive Officer SMD Ltd

"This system can be used in business, but also in your personal life. 90 Days to Profit takes you through a step-by-step system where you will find yourself going from problems to profit. Awesome!"

- Steven Essa
Millionaire Entrepreneur,
Real Estate Investor & #1 Bestselling Author

"I have worked with Steve on several occasions over the years and he is a delight to watch. The process that he uses is logical and remarkably easy to follow. That is one the main strengths of the 7 Steps. A lot of consultants feel like they have to prove that they are the smartest person in the room. Steve uses exactly the opposite approach by facilitating the informal teams to achieve fantastic results in a very short time. His book "90 Days to Profit" is a modern day version of "The Goal" by Eli Goldratt and I sincerely hope that it is just as successful. It deserves to be a classic".

- Mike Davies
CEO, Lean and Agile Ltd

"90 Days to Profit is the Pareto principle on hyperdrive, explained in a simple way I have never seen before. Frankly, it's required reading for business owners and executives. Read, implement and profit."

- Austin Netzley
Bestselling Author &
Founder of Epic Launch

"I have had the pleasure to work with Steve on a number of occasions in recent years and he has always delivered a successful outcome for the client in sometimes extremely high pressure situations. His new book "90 Days to Profit" is a well worked and detailed study of how he has been so successful over the years and I would recommend it to anyone who wants to transform their business in the shortest time"

- Simon Gough
Managing Partner Boyden Interim

"I worked with Steve at SMD and it was a very positive experience for me. I have seen the 7 Steps in action up close and personal and I know how effective it is. This process is simple yet powerful and if you follow it you will get a much better result for your business. If you add to that your own personal drive and experience you will have a winning combination"

- Mark Collins
Managing Director, SMD Ltd,
ROV Systems Division

ABOUT THE AUTHORS

Erlend Bakke is a Norwegian serial entrepreneur, #1 international bestselling author, popular podcast host, consultant, and speaker. He is a turnaround expert who helps companies go from loss to profits in 90 days or less. Having launched successful companies as a self-funded entrepreneur, he has an excellent grasp on what it takes to make businesses prosper in a competitive and  challenging environments when resources are scarce. His success places him in the top 7% of all entrepreneurs in the world. He knows what it takes to grow and transform businesses quickly and profitably. Today, he spends most of his time between Oslo and London.

 **Steve Shoulder** has grown businesses by up to 770% in one year using creative means to improve top line and bottom line growth. He is a business transformation expert with consistent international success in manufacturing, technology and service businesses. He has transformed dozens of underachieving companies by rebuilding their strategy, restructuring operations, increasing sales, raising output and productivity, reducing waste, improving product and process quality and positively impacting bottom line profitability. He is a subject matter expert in Lean Manufacturing methodologies and a

consummate team builder at all levels in a business. His success is driven by leadership, growth and return on investment. He is able to galvanise and energise management teams and get them all facing the right way in pursuit of clearly articulated and agreed targets.

Connect with us:
www.90daystoprofit.co.uk/

Contact us:
iwantprofits@90daystoprofit.co.uk

FOREWORD

In the 2007 movie 'Run, Fatboy, Run', Simon Pegg played a character called Dennis. Five years after jilting his pregnant fiancée on their wedding day, an out-of-shape Dennis decided to run a marathon to win her back – a seemingly impossible task given Dennis' physical condition and the short space of time available.

In a somewhat uninvited fashion, Dennis' landlord, Mr Goshdashtidar (played by Harish Patel), assumes the role of 'Assistant Coach' and on a number of occasions throughout the movie can be seen 'encouraging' Dennis with a large spatula and the question 'who the hell are you?'

You might be wondering about the relevance of this to the serious business of turnaround, transformation and indeed, to this book. I will explain later.

I first met – and then worked with – Steve Shoulder close to 20 years ago. Since then I have experienced his abilities first hand in a number of different situations and been lucky to have seen him deliver some outstanding business improvements.

You may well ask 'who the hell are you?' when you first meet Steve Shoulder. But whatever your first impression, it won't take you long to realise that Steve Shoulder is different - in approach, in outlook and most definitely, in results.

Steve approached me and asked if I would write a foreword to '90 Days To Profit' and I was delighted to be able to do this. The book presents a powerful methodology to bring about significant business improvement – in any number of situations. It is as relevant to survival turnaround as it is to accelerated growth.

I mentioned that Steve and I first met and worked together around 20 years ago. In fact this was in 1998, in a UK business providing cables and other network products and at that time facing an enormous expansion opportunity – offering us the chance to deliver a result well beyond the realms of what you might call 'a great year'. It was also an opportunity requiring a fresh outlook and unhindered ambition in order to get that result.

Steve joined us and during the following 12 months, together we made changes that allowed turnover to increase from £36m to £160m, with a thirty-fold increase in profit! This was absolutely unique, one of the most exciting periods in my working life and for me a pleasure to be part of such an incredible journey. It is not often that you get to do something like this in your working life and I was lucky to have such an opportunity.

So how did we do this and how does Steve deliver such great results?

Well, I knew that he had a very structured and effective way of transforming a business. I saw first-hand that not only does Steve have this very logical, thorough process – he leaves no stone unturned - but he also has a total focus on delivery.

One of the key things about the way that Steve does this kind of work is the way that he engages with teams and with management throughout the business. Not just with the individual that retained his services, as you might find in a traditional consultancy assignment, but truly across the entire spectrum of people within the organisation. He is a strong character ('who the hell are you?') but the way that he crafts a story and puts it across, it is very hard to say no to what he is proposing. Of course, reading about his methods in this book and how he builds that case, it is clear to me now that the processes I experienced while working with Steve were leading us all to the same conclusion so it was easy to say yes and to move forward confidently.

These experiences later led to Steve and I working together in improving other businesses, domestic and international, with equally positive results. As I look back on those times and I think about the way that the transformations took place and how it was all managed, I can now see all of the elements of the process and how they were used to such great effect. As I read '90 Days To Profit' now, I realise that perhaps back then I did not know the full system – but having taken in all the details and the subtlety, I can now understand much better how he was able to get such amazing results in such a short time frame.

I can honestly say that this process is remarkably effective.

If you are a senior business leader looking for a tried and proven way to transform your own business, then this book will definitely give you the tools and techniques you need to do that. Perhaps you are a consultant or aspiring to be a consultant. If that is the case, then you will learn a lot from the teachings in the book. If you really want to get the very best out of it, then I would suggest that you contact Steve directly and find out how he can either help your business or how he can train and coach you to become a top notch transformation professional. In either situation, you will be able to achieve what might seem impossible at the outset. A little like Dennis and his marathon.

It is always nice to meet and associate with people at the very top of their game. Steve is one of those people and I can guarantee if you put his teachings into practice, then you will also rise to the top.

I wish you every success on your own transformation journey.

Steve Ellis – International Business Leader, Main Board Member and, on occasions, 'Assistant Coach'

FREE BONUS MATERIAL

This book is dedicated to the people who want to turn around their business and maximize their profits. To help you achieve this goal in 90 days or less, we have created the following FREE bonus material to the book:

1. 7 in depth step-by-step tutorials on 90 Days to Profit

2. PDF resources and frameworks to use in your business

3. Access to Live Webinar where you can get direct access to the experts

To get the free book guide and get started on maximizing your profit using our proven 7 Steps to Profit system, please visit:
www.90daystoprofit.co.uk/bonus/

INTRODUCTION

It was a glorious spring day and I was standing on the roof of the BBC television centre in Manchester in front of the live broadcast cameras. My heart was thumping hard and my mind was racing. The producer counted us in.

"Three, two, one", and the BBC interviewer looked straight at the camera and said "Good morning and welcome. We are live from BBC News, Monday the 26th of April, with our main story: Millikan Automotive delivers record numbers for the first quarter. For the past twelve months, the business had been all over the media for the wrong reasons, with a massive backlog of orders and thousands of angry customers claiming they had no car to drive. Millikan have also had deeply troubled financial figures over the past two years. But now everything seems to have turned around. Here to explain the miracle of Millikan and how they went from loss to profit in 90 days is Ralph Hill, who has led the transformation. How did you make it all happen Ralph?"

Here we go, I thought, first time on national TV. I had never done this before but I was not going to let this opportunity get away from me. I smiled and said "Well, it all started by me getting fired and turning my own life around..".

On that beautiful spring day I was on top of the world. But three months earlier my world had been a very different place. You know you've hit rock bottom when you start drinking during the day and trying to hide it from your loved ones. I've been there. I know what it feels like to stay in bed the whole day because there is nothing to get up for. I know how it feels to examine every part of your life to try and find anything good about yourself. That is what losing your job does to your self-esteem. It takes away your identity and makes you question everything about your own sense of self-worth. I've also experienced what it feels like to be on top of the world. To be master of all I survey and know that I am unstoppable. Which one do you think I prefer? This is my story – a story of how I learned to positively transform any business in 90 days, but also the story of my own journey of transformation.

My name is Ralph Hill, and not so long ago everything seemed so secure. I'd graduated from university with a mechanical engineering degree and got a good job with a local engineering company. I worked my way up through the ranks to become one of the youngest managers in the company. And then out of the blue all of those years of effort unravelled in one afternoon – I was fired. The big chiefs said that I was a disruptive influence; that I was trying to make too many changes too quickly without getting their buy-in. I thought that was what they wanted – young, hungry managers who wanted to make positive change, but it seems I was wrong. At the time I was pretty damned angry about it all. After 10 years at the company I'd been dumped onto the street at a time of recession, when no-one was hiring, and my prospects looked grim. Looking back on it now, I can laugh at myself for the way I felt back then – because getting fired from that job was one of the best things that could ever have happened to me. It was the first, involuntary step in a process of change and learning that has led to me being more successful than I ever could have imagined. It has allowed me to meet some amazing people, and it has enabled me to learn one of the biggest secrets in the world of business – how to turn a failing company into a successful one in seven simple steps.

I tried to be enthusiastic when I first got fired even though it was a stressful time for me and my wife Maricel. I applied for jobs near and far, and told myself I would be sure to get something very quickly. But I found that due to the global recession and general uncertainty in the economy there were very few companies hiring at my level. After a discussion with a friend, I decided set myself up as a consultant and try to go it alone. But I quickly found that simply registering a business and giving yourself a job title doesn't actually bring the money in by itself. This was one of the lowest points in my life. I was depressed. Maricel was giving me a hard time. We could barely make ends meet any more on her salary alone. I even found myself starting to have the odd drink – or two, or three – during the day, "just to perk myself up a little". All in all, I was feeling pretty sorry for myself.

Then I had a lucky break. I was in a service station one afternoon filling up my car when I bumped into a guy I used to work with ten years earlier. Sam Newton was his name. Sam was a little older than me, and was someone I'd always looked up to when we worked together. He had been in the Special Forces prior to joining our company and he was as tough as they come. He had actually left the company to set himself up as a business consultant, taking the exact same path I was now trying to follow. I hadn't seen him since, but he was clearly doing very well for himself – he was driving a brand new, metallic blue Porsche Targa 911 and was dressed in designer clothes. Armani jeans! I didn't even know Armani made jeans. He was also wearing my all-time favourite watch, a Rolex GMT Master II in white gold. I was salivating just looking at it.

Sam was happy to see me again after all that time, and we got chatting over a coffee in the service station. I told him that I had been fired and that I was finding it difficult to get work as a consultant. I also admitted that I was not really confident that I could lead a consultancy assignment by myself, due to my lack of real world experience. Sam, on the other hand, told me that he had been going from strength to strength since going solo – he'd developed a unique methodology for transforming failing businesses, and was training other consultants to deliver it across the world. The difference between us seemed to be a yawning chasm, and I was starting to feel even more depressed about where my life had taken me. I was feeling like a victim, and that's a terrible place to be. I hate to hear people talking like victims, but I must have sounded like one myself that day.

That's when the miracle happened.

"I have always liked you, Ralph" said Sam, "and I'd like to help you". He said that he was running a training course starting that weekend for new and aspiring consultants. As a special favour, I could sign up even though the class was officially full, if I was really serious about being a great consultant. The fee for the course was £10,000 - way out of my league given my current circumstances. He looked at my face and said "I know what you are thinking Ralph. You are thinking that this course is not something that you can afford right now. Well, I can tell you that the best investment you will ever make is in yourself and your career – that is, if you believe in yourself. You can start the course on Saturday and you can pay me £5000 upfront and then another £5,000 in 6 weeks' time. I don't usually do this for anyone, so if I were you I would stop thinking about how you can't afford it, and work out what you can do to make it happen. If you start asking yourself better questions, you will get better answers".

I was in a turmoil. This sounded too good to be true. I was desperate to learn what Sam knew, but unsure of whether I could take such a financial risk. I asked "will this help me to get started in my new career, Sam? How will I find my clients? That is the bit that I am struggling with at the moment".

Sam smiled and said "Good things happen to people around me. My network is huge and growing every day. I will recommend good people to the clients I already know, and your confidence will do the rest. Also, if you attend the first session and you don't like it, you can finish up right then and I will return every penny you have paid" He held his hand out to shake on the deal. Impulsively, I grabbed it and shook it hard. "Good man, Ralph. I will see you at the Waterview Hotel at 8am on Saturday morning and we'll get started", Sam smiled.

I did not know it at the time but I was about to learn in a very real and practical way the secrets behind Sam's success. It is called the 7 Steps to Profit. It is the most powerful business transformation tool you could ever use and it consists of a structured way to work through virtually any business issue – from a small problem solving exercise, to transforming a whole business and more. The process is completely flexible and scalable to suit almost any situation. And best of all, it contains just seven simple steps, which you'll discover as you read this book - Problem, Review, Opportunity, Fine Tune, Implement and Test, Tracking, and Shape and Rollout. Together, they spell out what this system will achieve for you: PROFITS.

I was consumed by how I could find the money to pay for this course. I had my sports motorcycle, which I didn't really use enough these days to justify leaving it sitting in the garage, so I could sell that and it would pay the first £5,000. I had no idea how I would find the remaining money. I told Maricel what I had done when I got home and she couldn't believe that I had done something so rash. She gave me a really hard time.

"Honestly, Ralph, wouldn't it make more sense to try and get a proper job rather then doing this? You've been trying the consultancy thing out for months now, and it just hasn't been working out for you. How is spending ten grand that we don't even have going to improve things?"

I said "I have to find something that will break me out of this situation and this may well be it. I am going to take a chance on this and I would like your support".

She frowned and said "I guess I'm not going to change your mind on this one right now. I just hope it works out positively Ralph, because we're barely making ends meet as it is". I was beginning to doubt myself but my gut feeling was telling me that yes, this was the right thing for me to do. Sometimes in life you need to take a leap into the unknown and trust that faith will guide you in the right way.

Later that same day I advertised my bike on the internet to raise the first £5,000 and hoped to hell that I was doing the right thing for my career and for my marriage. I never thought that I would be in this position and it was totally new ground for me. I felt like the safe, cosy existence I once had was now being challenged in ways that I had never dreamed of, and it was not a pleasant experience. But I was determined to make my life better and this was the opportunity that I had in front of me so I was going for it. I remembered some ancient Stoic advice that my dad used to give me from Epictetus´s handbook: "some things are up to us and some are not up to us". There are things that we can control and there are other things that we can't. My actions, habits and focus are all elements that I have 100% control over and I felt firmly that taking action on Sam´s offer was right. I had a feeling that the course would not only teach me the skills I needed to be a transformation specialist, but also transform my own life and fortunes at the same time. I only hoped that I was doing the right thing as there was so much at stake here. My financial future hung in the balance. My marriage was taking a battering. My reputation was on the line if I was not successful, and when I thought about it like that and put myself in Maricel's place – well, maybe I could see her point of view. But risky or not, I was in it now, and I was not going to back out.

7 STEPS TO PROFIT

1 Problems

CHAPTER ONE

P IS FOR PROBLEMS
SAM'S SESSION 1

I turned up at the hotel on Saturday morning to find 20 other people already waiting. They'd all paid £10,000 for this course of seven sessions over the next three months. Quite a time commitment, but one which they were clearly all prepared to make, and I figured there must be a good reason for that. Soon, Sam arrived and the seminar began. He welcomed us to the course and then said "Before we start can I get you all some water?" A few of us said yes so Sam picked up a glass jug and came over to the first guy on my left. He lifted a glass off the table and started to pour. But he didn't stop, and the water started spilling out all over the floor. The guy jumped up in shock. Sam stopped and looked around. He raised an eyebrow and said "You all know what this means, right?" I thought I knew, and said "Is it the parable of the empty cup?"

Sam nodded. "Empty your cup" is said to come from a conversation between scholar Tokusan and Zen Master Ryutan in the 8th century. Tokusan, who was so full of knowledge and opinions, came to Ryutan to ask him about Zen. At one point Ryutan re-filled the teacup of Tokusan, but he didn't stop pouring when the cup was full, and the tea spilled out and ran over the table. "Stop! The cup is full!" said Tokusan. "Exactly, Tokusan," said Master Ryutan. "You are like this cup; you are so full of ideas. You come to me and ask for teaching, but your cup is full; I can't put anything in. Before I can teach you, you have to empty your cup". Sam went on to explain that this is much harder than you might realize. By the time we reach adulthood we are so full of conventional wisdom, preconceived notions, and filters and limitations of various kinds that we don't even notice them. We might consider ourselves to be open minded, but in fact everything we learn is filtered through many assumptions and then classified to fit into the knowledge we already possess.

Sam then gave us his version of the empty cup. He told it like this:

"Have you ever started to learn something and thought after a very short while that you already know this stuff? Have you then just skimmed over the rest of it and not really taken it all in?" We all shifted in our seats a little. He said "Don't worry, this is exactly what 99.9% of the population do every day. You are not going to be in that number. You are going to be in the 0.1% who actually open their mind and take in learning properly, so that you can use it to achieve great things. If you catch yourself thinking that you already know something, stop and give yourself a mental slap. Wake yourself up to what is in front of you. Unless you are a 10 year veteran of this particular subject of knowledge the chances are that you only have a very shallow and tenuous understanding of the material. Go with the flow and open your heart and mind to the concepts we are about to learn. Genuinely learn not just the theory but also the practice. When you learn something new in this course you should immediately go and apply it in practice. That is when you really get to know how well you have learned. The future of the business and all of the people in it are relying on your grasp of this material, so it had better be good". He looked really serious for a moment or two, then cracked a smile and said brightly "no pressure then!" We all laughed nervously, but we knew the importance of this lesson. We had to become expert practitioners in just seven sessions, and to do that we had to genuinely open up our hearts and minds and learn like a child again.

Sam then said "Okay, now let's really get started. The course that I am about to take you through is a proven system that you will learn and implement as you go along. It is called "7 Steps to Profit" for reasons that will become clear to you as we go through the material. I will be using military metaphors and examples as we go through this course because it is a very large part of my background and so much of it applies almost perfectly to business situations. A lot of people think that the military is all about command control, and to be fair there used to be a lot of that sort of thing in the past. Nowadays it is much more about teamwork and being smart. This whole course is based around the word PROFITS and each session will take one of those letters and make it into a meaningful learning framework. So what does P stand for?" he asked.

"Well, Sam, I thought that was what you're here to tell us", volunteered one of the attendees. Another nervous laugh rippled among us.

"Well, you thought wrong", replied Sam calmly. "I'm not here to tell you things, I'm here to show you how to think for yourselves. And more importantly, how to do things for yourselves – when you go out and do a job for yourself, you remember almost 100% of what you learn; when you sit around reading a text and nothing else, you pick up 30% at most. That's why it's important that you all either have an assignment or are actively pursuing prospects. Think of me as someone who is going to guide you through the process of learning, rather than like your old university lecturer who liked to listen to himself talk. It might seem a little unusual at first, but I think you'll get the hang of it quickly enough, and I know you'll see the benefits by the time we're done. Now, just imagine yourself in a critical situation in a business – what would be the first thing you'd do?"

After bouncing some ideas back and forth Sam told us that in step one, P is for Problem. At the start of every assignment you have to first figure out what problem you are going to solve. He said it was like the first part of every military campaign. You are given a mission by your superiors and you are then faced with working out what it is you need to tackle. He said "Suppose you have been told by your commanding officer that you have to rescue a very important general who has been taken prisoner by the enemy. Do you just jump into your armoured car and drive off into the sunset hoping for a good result? Of course not. But that is exactly what a lot of people in business do. They think they know the answer instinctively and they just start doing things. There is a better way.

"First you understand everything there is to know about where the general is, who is holding him, what are the traps and obstacles, the terrain, the ambush points, the fall back positions and a hundred other things before you can fully understand what you are facing. You are defining the "Problem" which is the P in the 7 Steps to Profit. The key part of step one is for everyone involved to agree on the problem before you move forward. You need to get your experienced officers and sergeants around the table and all agree on what the mission is going to be before you make a single move forward. Then you run it past your commanding officer to let him buy-into it and give you the go ahead to proceed with the mission.

"It is exactly the same in business. You need to very clearly define the problem you are going to fix before you do anything. There are always 500 potential problems to fix in every business, but you need to focus very tightly on one or two well-articulated key problems so that you can direct all of your resources into getting the best possible result in the shortest possible time".

Sam went on to suggest spending 15 minutes every morning doing nothing but thinking quietly to ourselves about what needs to be done that day. Just sit with a pad and a pencil in a quiet place and put your mind in neutral and think about the things that are happening in the business and what you can do that day to have the biggest impact. There are no limits, and you allow your mind to make seemingly unconnected things come together. He said that this exercise alone had helped him to solve many issues that the previous day had seemed impossible. Even in the middle of a stressful day, the simple act of sitting quietly for fifteen minutes in your car or the canteen could help to clear things up. I was learning so much in this first session that my head felt like the opposite of an empty cup already – it was ready to burst!

At the end of the first session we all intimately understood step one of the 7 Steps to Profit System which is to identify and agree what problem needs to be fixed. This agreement needs to include the whole business before you make a start on any improvement work. Sam quoted Peter Drucker, who said this about all good managers: "They know that they have no choice but to do first things first and second things not at all".

I guess what he was saying is that it is very easy to do something but not so easy to do the one thing that will make the difference. I did not forget that quote and I could see that in the past I had been guilty of working on things that would make no difference at all. We have all done it; we just need to be honest about it and admit what we have done and how we are going to act differently in the future.

We were now ready to get back into the real world and start to use the information we had learned. In between sessions we had to practice what we had learned so that it became part of our useable knowledge base very quickly. But I was still an unemployed consultant – how was I going to implement any of this? But as I packed up to leave, Sam approached me with a lead to follow up. He said "Ralph I know a banker called Simon Brown who's looking for a consultant right now, he needs to transform a high profile local business which is struggling. I would do it myself, but I just don't have the time right now, and he needs someone urgently. Here's the details," he said, passing me a business card with a few notes scribbled hastily on the back. "Give him a call this afternoon, but only if you're genuinely interested".

I took the card and said "A banker working on a Saturday?" Sam smiled and said "Simon is not your average banker – he'll take your call today".

My First Assignment

I could barely keep calm as I walked to my car. I called Simon straight away and, sure enough, he answered. I introduced myself and told him that Sam had asked me to call him. Simon invited me to see him later that same day, and when I arrived he wasted no time in coming to the point. He got me to sign a confidentiality agreement, and then told me that Millikan Electric Vehicles was the company in question, which astonished me. They had a fantastic product, a really high-end luxury electric vehicle, sort of like an electric-powered Bentley. Simon explained that they had a full order book going out two to three years, so they had plenty of work in front of them; but they couldn't produce the vehicles quickly enough to cover their weekly costs, and were therefore running at a loss despite a seemingly booming business. This was to be expected at their stage of development to a certain extent, but they were 2,000 vehicles behind their forecast and their customers were getting edgy. He asked me a few questions about what I had done in the past and he seemed happy with what he heard – obviously my background as an employee was enough to disguise my lack of consultancy experience, at least this time.

He said "That sounds great Ralph, and if you're being trained by Sam Newton then you're probably someone who can help to pull them out of this mess. You can start on Monday. I will let them know you are coming. I cannot put too fine a point on this Ralph – you only have 90 days to get this business turned around. I am getting all kinds of pressure from my directors so I need a result here". He was deadly serious.

I asked him about my day rate for the assignment and he said "I was thinking of £1250 a day Ralph. It isn't top dollar, but I'm taking a chance on you based on Sam's recommendation. You okay with that?"

Inside I was delighted – that was significantly more than I had ever earned before, but I remembered to play it cool. I said "That rate seems fine to me. Could you also consider a bonus based on the improved value of the business after the 90 days – assuming that it's back on the right track at that stage?"

He looked at me a bit sideways and said "You definitely take after Sam. Yes, I will consider that. If you can work some magic and get this business turned around, it'll be worth a lot of money to this bank. We will come up with a suitable number when you get there".

I smiled and said "I trust you on that one, Simon. Sam told me that you were a person that would honour his word". Simon smiled and we shook on it.

"Incidentally, you may want to check out the latest edition of Fortune magazine" he added. "It features the Millikan founder Leon Musket. It'll give you some idea of who you will be dealing with".

I dived into the article about Leon Musket that same evening, and did some of my own research into the business press. Millikan's owner was a maverick entrepreneur called Leon Musket, a larger-than-life South African who was seen as a technological visionary, but clearly one who didn't know how to run a factory to get the best output. The result was that Millikan was struggling to survive despite having a very full order book. The workforce was pulled from the local area, which was rich in highly skilled workers left over from the traditional industries that used to be in the region. There were lots of traditional coachbuilders and tradesmen ready to take up the jobs in the factory, who were very skilled but quite old-fashioned in their ways.

The bank had already sent in two big-name consultancies and they had both recommended that the business loans be foreclosed. The banks and other investors had very large loans and a sizeable overdraft facility with this business, amounting to more than £100m, and they didn't want to lose their money, so drafting me in was a last-chance gamble to avoid that. If I couldn't work out a way to save this business in 90 days, the bank would foreclose and 1300 local jobs and an industry icon would be lost. No pressure.

When I got home that afternoon I told Maricel that I had won my first assignment. She was amazed at how quickly this had happened. I told her all about the meeting and she was impressed at the day rate and the possibility of a big bonus at the end if it all went well. However, she was always the practical type: "All of this sounds really great Ralph. But you know how we are fixed financially. It is really great that you have landed an assignment so quickly, but do you think you're maybe jumping in at the deep end here? Two consultants with a lot more experience than you have already tried and failed to fix this. I'm willing to support you on this for a little longer, but I still think it might be safer to have a back-up option – I can ask around my office and see if there's anything going. If we could get you a steady full-time job for a bit it would really help to pull us out of our financial difficulties first, then you could focus on the consultancy on the side".

I was a little offended at what I perceived to be her lack of support – she didn't think I could hack it, and she wanted me to go back to the 9-to-5. I mumbled a maybe towards her suggestion, then continued talking about the role at Millikan. When I was finished, I could see she still wasn't completely convinced.

"Maricel" I said, "this is a great opportunity for me to turn my life around and it is the only option on the table right now. I'm going to succeed".

The fact that I clearly believed in myself placated her a little, but she quietly read a magazine for most of the evening while I watched a little television and had a couple of beers to unwind after a stressful but exciting day.

Problem Identification

This was new ground for me, and it took all I had to suppress the nerves when I turned up at the Millikan reception on Monday morning. Just as I was signing into the visitor's book, I heard a booming voice behind me.

"You must be Ralph Hill – are you?"

I turned around and saw a very large, well-dressed man coming towards me. His face was grim, but he held his head high and had a swagger in the way that he walked. He reached out his hand and squeezed mine ridiculously hard while twisting it slightly anti-clockwise to show who was in charge.

"I'm Paul Howard," he said quietly, "Sales Director here at Millikan. I've built this business from the ground up alongside Leon, and I am damned if I am going to let any consultants come in here and try to close us down". He'd obviously been waiting for me.

My heart was pounding, but I returned his gaze. "Yes, I'm Ralph. Very pleased to meet you, Paul. I have heard about your fantastic success with Millikan, and I can assure you that I am only here to help and to get a great result for the business". He seemed to soften just a touch. He suddenly turned and began pacing back down the corridor, shouting over his shoulder at me, "Come with me, I'll show you where you can sit". After showing me into an empty meeting room, he said "Brian Conroy will come over to show you around. Take a seat".

Looking around, the room had a central table made from Japanese maple that would seat 20 people. The chairs were top quality and there was a huge TV screen at the end of the room, presumably for presentations and video conferencing. Very impressive. I plugged in and got myself set up.

Brian Conroy was a short, stocky guy with a neatly trimmed beard, a smile on his face and a twinkle in his eye. He shook my hand when he arrived and said "I'm Brian Conroy, Production Manager at Millikan. I have been building vehicles of various kinds all my working life. I joined Millikan 5 years ago when they were just starting out and I can do every job on the shop floor because I designed most of the processes myself".

"That's quite an opening line" I said, and smiled. "Paul Howard said that you would show me around. Are you ready to go?"

"Sure, come with me and we will have a good look around and meet some of our people" said Brian.

We passed by a few offices before Brian walked into one of them. He said "This is the Procurement Office, these guys are absolutely rushed off their feet every day. I will introduce you to the Procurement Manager, he's a good guy". We made our way over to the end of the room, to a separate glass-fronted office where a young man sat at a desk with his eyes glued to a screen.

Brian walked in and said "Allan Matthews, meet Ralph Hill". Allan smiled and stood up. He must have been six-and-a-half feet tall and, like a lot of very tall guys, he had a tendency to stoop. He also had a friendly face touched with a bit of worry.

He stretched out his hand and said "Hi Ralph, pleased to meet you. I knew you were coming, word gets around very quickly here. I hope you can make some sense of all of this pretty quickly, because we're disappearing up our own exhaust pipe, if you know what I mean?"

I shook his hand and said "Nice to meet you too, Allan. Though I don't think electric vehicles have an exhaust pipe". This broke the ice nicely. I continued "I'll come back and talk to you when you have a bit of time for me".

"No worries Ralph, just pop by any time. If I am not with anyone you can just come in and we'll talk" said Allan.

We carried on down the corridor and met with the CFO, Martin Kirkbride. Martin also seemed like a decent guy and he looked like the archetypal accountant, tall and wiry with a shiny bald head, piercing blue eyes and horn-rimmed glasses. Straight away I liked him a lot. He was very worried about the financial state of the business, and said that whatever numbers I wanted I should just come and ask him and he would sort me out.

I followed Brian out of the office and down a long flight of stairs to another office. He said "This is the production office where I normally sit, and you will find the supervisors and planners in here as well. Let me introduce you to Mal Davies". He walked up to the middle of the office where a dark, swarthy guy with thick forearms and heavy black rimmed glasses was sitting in front of a window that looked out onto the shop floor. Brian said "Mal, meet Ralph Hill".

Mal stood and we shook hands. He had a very strong handshake and hard skin, like a man who was used to working with his hands. He said "Pleased to meet you Ralph. We all knew you were coming this morning. The jungle drums work exceptionally well around here". I'd heard words like these before, and I knew I was in a place that had good communications and was open and honest in its dealings with people at all levels. This was another very good sign that they had retained the start-up mentality and positivity.

"Pleased to meet you too Mal," I replied, "I will probably need to be talking to you a fair bit over the next few days, so I hope you can spare me some time".

Mal replied "I spend a lot of time on the shop floor so best to come and find me either in here or out there when you want to talk". I thanked him, and we moved back upstairs and further down the corridor to the last door on the right.

The door was open and Brian stuck his head in. "Leon, are you free to meet with Ralph Hill, the new consultant?"

I heard a distinctive South African voice say "Sure, come on in, but I only have a few minutes".

This was the visionary himself, the legendary entrepreneur Leon Musket. I was expecting to see someone with surrounded by hi-tech computer gadgetry, working on about seven screens at once. But his work set up was much less cluttered than that. There were two desks, however. One was a normal height desk, with an ergonomic office chair behind it. It was empty. Leon was instead working at a walking desk with a monitor set into the ergonomic inner frame. He was literally walking at a treadmill while doing his work! The surprise on my face must have been obvious, as Brian nudged me and said "just one of Leon's many eccentricities". He gave me a wink as Leon switched off the treadmill and stepped back onto firm ground.

Leon walked over to shake hands, making eye contact as he did so. "Nice to meet you Ralph," said Leon, "and welcome to Millikan. Paul Howard told me that you were here. I hope you can help us to get the place buzzing". He had a quick and energetic way of talking, but his calm eyes stayed on you the whole time, making you feel like the centre of his attention.

I replied "Thank you Mr Musket" to which he immediately insisted I call him Leon, before I continued "I'm very pleased to be here, and looking forward to helping out. I met with Paul Howard in reception when I first arrived and he showed me where to get set up".

"Don't you worry about Paul. He's a big dog in this place, but his bark is worse than his bite, I can tell you. He is a tough negotiator though, and the best sales director we could ever wish for. He'll get behind you when he sees you making progress. So, tell me, how do you plan to go about this Ralph?"

This was the question I had been waiting for since Saturday. Sam's first seminar had taught me exactly how to respond. I said "I am going to spend the first one to two weeks getting to understand what is really going on in the business. I am going to speak to people at all levels, including yourself and your senior team, all the way through the organisation right down to the shop floor. I am going to watch and observe and ask all the relevant questions. I will get the high level numbers and speak with Martin Kirkbride to understand and interpret them, and at the end of that I will be in a position to suggest to you the one most important thing that we need to fix. I am not going to change anything until I have agreement from you on that".

Leon smiled and said "Ralph, you're a straight talker, and I like that. Your plan sounds great to me, and I think we're going to get along just fine. Come back and talk to me when you are ready. I would like a weekly update by email as a minimum on your progress. Just let me know what you have done in the week, what you are planning to do, any challenges you are facing, and any opportunities you have spotted. But if my door is open, you feel free to come in anytime and we can have a discussion". The open door policy was clearly alive and well in Millikan.

Upon leaving, Brian added "There is one other guy that you should meet before we get much further into the day and that is Tommy Sherwin, the full-time union official".

Tommy Sherwin's office had a sign that read 'TGWU Official' in solid black letters on a white background. Brian knocked and waited. This was the first time that we had come across a closed door and also the first time that Brian had knocked. A voice gruffly said "Come in", and he opened the door. To the left was a large desk and sat behind the desk was a large, heavy built guy with a totally bald head and 3 days growth of grey beard. He was wearing steel rimmed glasses too small for his head. He looked up and said "How can I help you Brian?"

Brian replied in his usual manner "Tommy Sherwin, meet Ralph Hill, the new consultant". Tommy stood up and stayed behind the desk. He reached out his hand to shake across the desk.

"Pleased to meet you" I said.

Tommy replied "I am not sure if I am pleased to meet you yet Ralph. I will let you know when I have had a chance to see what you want to do and how you want to do it. My members work very hard and I am here to make sure they get fairly treated and fairly rewarded for what they do".

"Tommy, we both have the same interests at heart. I want to help in making this business healthy and giving it a great future. You'll be consulted at every step of the process to make sure we are on the right track".

Tommy squinted and said gruffly "Sounds good Ralph, I'll make sure you stick to your word".

After leaving Tommy's office, Brian asked me "How about a look around the shop floor?" So I got kitted out with all of the necessary safety gear and we headed out onto the floor to see the whole process from goods inwards to finished product delivery. I was struck by the old-fashioned nature of the build process – this was not a totally modern car assembly plant. Some parts were state of the art and other parts were like a cottage industry. The whole product ethos was based around a 'hand built quality' theme, a very slow process with obvious opportunities for improvement.

When I got back to my office I wrote up my notes. I wrote down what I saw, what people had told me and, in particular, what I had learned from Brian. It was impressive to hear Brian talking about every part of the process in such detail. It was clear that he knew it intimately and he was proud of where the company had come from and how much progress it had made. The first sketch I drew was to set out the key members of staff I would be working with in four different areas of the business.

The second drawing was to understand the business in more intricate detail and to more clearly understand what functions were going on in the business itself and where my focus areas might be:

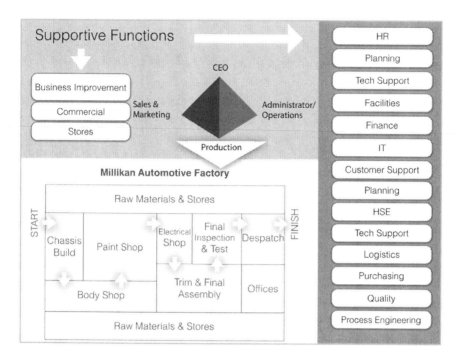

It was also very useful for me to get insights into what made people tick. There is politics in every business no matter how big or small, and it pays to know your allies as well as your opponents. It also pays to know how to get people lined up behind your proposals so that you get the least amount of resistance. It was clear for me that Brian would be a big help with this.

I sketched out the production process quickly and came up with a page that looked something like this:

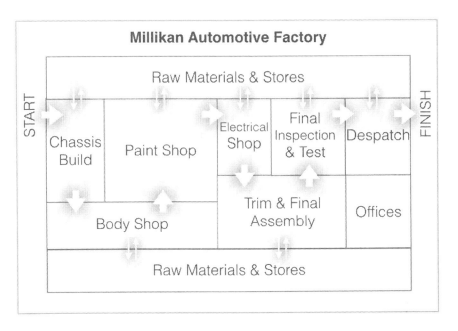

Millikan Automotive Factory

I put some numbers into this basic diagram and discovered very quickly that the process was really unbalanced. There were areas that were coping easily with the demand they faced, and other areas where they needed to run an extra shift to just about keep pace with demand. This led to all kinds of blockages and shortages, especially when there was a breakdown or other kind of stoppage and there were lots of opportunities to improve it with very little investment. This gave me some ideas about where to start. I could also see that there was lots of work in progress (WIP) in certain areas, which was a sure sign that the area was not keeping up with the rest of the factory in terms of flow rate. When the production flow in a factory is not steady, it creates a bottleneck. It was clear to me that the WIP was created because of some key areas that were slower or more dysfunctional in the factory.

I could visualise the whole manufacturing process as a human body, where all of the processes going on were important and interlinked. If you altered one function it would ultimately have an impact on the rest of the system. As each vehicle moved through the process it gained value, but it also picked up additional material cost, labour cost and overhead cost and the longer it took to get through the whole process the more expensive it became. The trick to this was getting each vehicle moving through the process more quickly so that it attracted less cost while still gaining value. Also, in the same way that a living organism would be treated for various ailments, it always made sense to not only treat the individual symptoms but also the whole organism so that a synergistic result was achieved. For now, I would need to identify which big domino was to be focused on first to dramatically slow down the illiquidity of the business. I was really getting into this.

I was absolutely buzzing when I was driving home that night. It had been a really long first day but a good one. I was pleased that I was getting into it so quickly and seeing lots of opportunities all over the business. I was looking forward to telling Maricel all about my day when I noticed that the house was dark. I was wondering what had happened when it hit me. I had arranged to have a celebratory dinner with Maricel to celebrate my first day in the new role and had completely forgotten about it.

When I got into the house the dining table was all set for a romantic dinner and there was a note propped up against one of the candlesticks. It read "Ralph, I gave up waiting at 9pm, you said that you would be home at 6:30. I have to be at work early so please sleep in the spare bedroom. Enjoy the dinner".

I was feeling like a complete jerk. How could I do this to her after all we had been through these last few months? I made a solemn promise to myself that I would make it up to her later in the week. I might be learning a lot about business but I still had a lot to learn about relationships. Maricel is the love of my life and I had to keep her engaged and motivated just like the people in the business. I told myself that I was not going to let Maricel down again any time soon and I would definitely make it up to her big style. I also made a mental promise to myself to get into better shape and to stop drinking. This was going to be an interesting few months for me. I was going on a journey of discovery in my professional life and now I was also highly motivated to go through a personal transformation.

Consensus Building

The following morning I got into work early and hunted down Brian to discuss the ideas and the process map that I'd developed the previous day. We talked about the possibility of rebalancing the process and dramatically reducing the amount of Work In Progress (WIP) that was sitting idle on the shop floor. This would potentially have a number of positive effects:

1. It would free up cash for the business

2. It would reduce the lead time per vehicle

3. It would improve overall output

4. It would reduce the cost per vehicle if it was done correctly

Brian was excited to see these possibilities in front of us. I asked if he and Mal could gather some top-level insights during the course of the day so that I could get some traction quickly. "Speak to as many key people as you can and just ask them these three questions," I said, "and make a note of their responses". I handed Brian a sheet with the questions written on it.

They were:

1. What is stopping you from hitting your targets?

2. What is frustrating you?

3. What would you like to change?

Brian took the questions and said "These look like pretty straightforward questions. People will be able to answer without fear of saying the wrong thing, and it will start to flush out the main issues".

"Yes," I replied, "it is a good opening set of questions and it will get people talking. Ask anyone who you think is a key person. It doesn't have to be only senior managers or supervisors, just anyone who will give you a considered answer. And try to cover as many departments in the business as you can. I'll start with the senior managers and work my way out to the factory and other areas". Brian agreed with this approach and said he would speak to Mal shortly.

Later that day I talked to the procurement manager, Allan Mathews, who told me that his daily workload felt like a constant juggling act. There was no proper means to ensure that all of the parts were available at the right place at the right time. Every vehicle was treated as a mini-project rather than a product on a production line, because this was what Leon thought the process should be. The appeal of having a high quality, hand-built, electric-powered luxury vehicle was what he had built the business on, and he wanted to keep it that way. But the workers on the shop floor were so far behind that they would constantly swap vehicle identities – what started as a car for a particular customer would end up being swapped to another customer with a different specification, because the right parts just happened to be available for that spec at the time! The whole planning and scheduling process was in total disarray. There had to be a way to improve it.

After that I spoke to the CFO, Martin Kirkbride and got as many facts and figures from him as possible, going as far back as he could manage. The labour and material costs, the gross margin, the overheads, the net margin, everything I could get my hands on. The end result of analysing all those figures was stark – the company needed to be producing around 100 completed vehicles per week just to break even, and they were only producing around 65 on average. I quickly did some numbers in my head. That means they are 2340 cars short a year and because this had been happening for a while they were likely short by around 4000 cars or more! Producing only 65% of what was needed to simply break even clearly explained why the bank desperately needed to see improvements to the business or foreclose on their loans. Millikan would need to increase production to around 150 cars to be a prosperous company which meant nearly tripling current production rates. I had my work cut out for me and I was wondering how many other people in the business actually knew this.

I headed over to Leon's office. His door was open. "Are you free for a few minutes Leon?" I asked.

Leon looked up and smiled. "Sure Ralph, come on in". He gestured towards a seat. "So what have you got for me?" I told him what I'd found, and what my first impressions were. I told him that instinctively it looked like we had to improve output and at the same time reduce WIP and free up the cash in the business. His initial reaction was positive as he took a long sip of a swamp-like green smoothie that sat on his desk. He swallowed and said: "Ralph, you have come a very long way in a really short time and I like what you have done. But whichever way this goes, I want you to keep in mind that the customer always comes first. That's a deal breaker for me. If you can find a way to make the process slicker, produce more vehicles, or reduce capital, that's great; but the quality has to stay the same, or even improve. I won't take anything less. I am happy for you to continue. Just keep me in the loop as to what you are doing and if you need any guidance or help, please come and talk to me". In these words I saw the intensity and determination that had made him into a famous entrepreneur; but I also knew that if we didn't make changes fast, he soon wouldn't have a business at all!

Overall I was pleased with Leon's reaction, but at the same time I had a slight sinking feeling – how was I going to make the radical changes the company needed in only 90 days while still maintaining a very high level of quality? I took a few deep breaths to compose myself, and started heading back to my office. A short way from there, I saw Paul Howard the sales director, coming along the corridor towards me. He stopped and asked how I was getting along, but when I started to give him the full rundown, he interrupted me and snapped "I don't need War and Peace, just tell me what you have been doing and where you're going with it". He was no more impressed by the short version than he was by the long version. He leaned forward as I had seen him do on the first day I arrived at Millikan and he said softly "I expected a lot better than this Hill, and I hope that you start making some real progress pretty quickly. I don't buy generalities and stories, I buy facts and figures. This may be the start and end of your consulting career if you don't lift your game". And with that he turned and walked back to his office. I can honestly say that he really got to me at that moment. I was feeling great after I had talked to Leon and now I was filled with self-doubt and wondering what the next few days would bring. I had to find a way to get Paul Howard behind this project, but I could already see that it was not going to be easy. These dark thoughts were in my mind as I drove home.

Nevertheless, I woke up the next morning in good spirits and was looking forward to a good day with the team. I had been reading up on the swamp water green smoothies Leon seemed to be constantly consuming, as I was drawn to how full of energy he was at all times. I wanted more energy at work and in life in general, and figured that if a busy and successful person like Leon has a system that works for him I could borrow from it to get the same results. I remembered a quote I had read from Tony Robbins, who said: "Long ago, I realized that success leaves clues, and that people who produce outstanding results do specific things to create those results. I believed that if I precisely duplicated the actions of others, I could reproduce the same quality of results that they had".

According to my research on green smoothies, what we eat and drink dramatically affects our bloods PH level. When we consume acidic foods and drinks like soda and fry-ups it takes our body a lot of energy to process and maintain a healthy PH level. When we eat foods with high alkalinity, however, our body spends a lot less energy on processing the food and maintaining the correct PH level. Ah-ha, I thought, that swamp water Leon drinks gives him energy instead of giving him that heavy feeling after lunch! I had gotten up early and brewed my first smoothie and was ready to get to work fully energized.

When I got to work I dropped off my bag in the office and found Brian Conroy at his desk – he was another early riser.

"Morning Brian, can we talk about our plans for the rest of this week?"

"Sure," replied Brian "I am looking forward to that"

I smiled at him. I liked Brian and I knew that we would make a good team on this project

He said "Shall I bring Mal Davies over as well and we can decide what we are going to get done?"

"Sounds good, let's go and see where he is"

Ten minutes later, we were sat around the meeting table in my office and I got things started. "We've all taken a lot of notes from our discussions and observations these last few days. I have made a summary of what we covered and I have collated it all into a number of themes and categories. It is clear that there are some common issues starting to emerge around raising output, freeing up cash within the business, balancing the process flow, making sure that we have all parts available for all vehicles before we launch the works orders, and a few other complementary issues".

Brian agreed. "Yes, that sounds about right. The same issues seemed to be coming up again and again".

Mal added "Getting the flow right so that we can produce more vehicles in less time and with less WIP seems to be the biggest issue from what I have seen and heard. Shall we put together an action plan detailing all the things we need to fix?" Mal was definitely a doer!

"Not yet Mal," I said, "I want to be sure that we get buy-in at all levels before we move forward. It's critical that we all get behind the change program from day one. And we need to keep a narrow laser focus so that we are only fixing one thing at a time, or it will start to run away from us".

"What do you suggest then Ralph?" asked Brian.

"I suggest that we all go back round to the key people in the business today and get complete consensus of what we are going to fix. We can feed back to them what we have found so far, and we can ask them another very specific set of questions".

Mal said "Is it really necessary to go through that again, it seems very similar to what we've done for the past two days?"

But I knew that Sam's method was the right one to use, so I replied "Mal, I appreciate your concern – but it's vital that we have complete agreement at all levels of the business before we start trying to put together a firm plan".

Mal demurred, and asked what kind of questions we should be asking this time.

I got up and went to the white board and picked up one of my notes from Sam´s first session. I asked "How about these?" and wrote:

1. Do you agree with the themes and issues we have uncovered so far?

2. Is there anything we have missed?

3. Is there anything you would change in regards to output and balancing the process flow?

4. If there is one thing above all else that we need to fix right now what would it be?

5. What is stopping us from fixing it right now?

6. What would enable us to fix it right now?

Mal was now beaming. He said "That looks brilliant, actually, I see where you're coming from now. This is making sure that we are on the right track and that we are bringing the people on the journey with us.

We will also flush out the really big issues and identify the blockers and enablers. You are pretty good at this stuff, Ralph".

We divided between us the list of key people we needed to speak to. "We can meet back here after lunch and compare notes," I suggested.

On the way back to my office I noticed Paul Howard speaking to one of the sales guys. I waited a moment until he had finished then walked up to Paul and said "Good morning Paul, how are you?

"Fine thanks Ralph" he replied, "It was good to spend some time with the grandkids last night. I trust we're going to see some rapid progress for the rest of this week?"

I smiled at him and said "I'm sure of it. We will agree on the main issue to be fixed and we will start to communicate our intentions to the staff. This is going to be a good few days. On that note, I would like to get your advice on a few things. Do you have some time this afternoon?"

Paul Howard softened visibly and said "Oh, of course. Drop by my office around 3pm and we can chat".

I headed back to my office with a spring in my step. Maybe I was going to make some headway with Paul after all.

When I went back to the office I took a moment to gather my thoughts, I realised that this morning we had created an informal team consisting of me, Brian, and Mal, and I sensed that this was one of the keys to getting a good result. I picked up my safety gear, as I knew that I would need to go into the factory to see some of the people on my list. I had about 15 people to see in 4 hours so I had to get a shimmy on and quickly calculated that I had about a quarter of an hour per person and I would try to get through as many as I could before lunch. I was almost skipping as I went out into the factory.

After lunch we met up again in Brian's office. We were buzzing with what we had achieved today and we were keen to share. I took the lead and said "Okay guys, we have all got some good stuff here. How should we go about summarising it all?"

Brian said "Well how about we go through the results for each person and you write them up on the whiteboard?"

I grabbed a marker and went to the board. I said "First up did any of the people we spoke to disagree with our findings so far?" Brian and Mal both shook their heads. "Did any of them say that we had missed anything or need to change anything?" Again they shook their heads. Brian said "It was not so much that they disagreed with any of it they just had a different idea as to what was the top priority and we can cover that when we do the writing up". I was happy with this and I started to write. I drew 3 columns with headings like this:

To Fix	Blockers	Enablers

Once the headings were in place Brian started to shout out the name of the person, the main issue to fix, any things that were blocking us from making that fix, and any things that were needed to enable it. I was busily scribbling away until Brian had finished and then Mal did the same thing for his list and my list. I kept a running tally of issues that came up more than once. After a solid half hour of writing and shouting out results we had a table which looked like this:

To Fix	No:	Blockers	No:	Enablers	No:
Output	9	Parts not available at the right time	11	Production line simulation	5
Cash Flow	5	Shortages on works orders	3	Golden rules for planning	11
Parts availability	8	Too much WIP	6	No works order issued with shortages	10
Process flow/design	5	Identity of orders locked in too early	4	Line balancing and process design	5
Line balancing	5	Mismatch of shifts and poor flow	7	Balance and match the shifts	3
Too much WIP	5	No golden rules for planning	5	Late customisation	6
Too much choice /customisation	4	Too many "options" and complexity	5	Not enough sub assembly build	6
Too many unfinished orders	4	Too many production slots for build	7	Reduce number of production slots	4
Cost reduction	6	Working capital tied up in WIP	9	Create buffer stocks with suppliers	3
Working capital reduction	3	No visibility of cash tied up in WIP	3	Poor performance metrics – visibility	6
Performance management	4	Poor performance due to shortages	2	Better communication of results	2
Poor planning	3	Planning is impossible in this situation	1	Input from shop floor into process	2
Purchasing and planning not aligned	3	Poor relationship with suppliers	1	Creative problem solving methods	1
Totals	64		64		64

Once this was written up and laid out in front of us it became clear that there was a lot of common ground between what people thought needed to be fixed and what was a blocker or an enabler.

I said "Guys, this is looking really promising. I think we need to prioritise this information, to rank the issues in order. How about I give that a go and we get back together a bit later to discuss it?"

The other two agreed that this was a sensible way forward and I headed back to my office where I could start to create a much shorter list with some sort of priority to it. I decided to take 15 minutes of thinking time to get clear on what was really going on. When I came back to my office I closed my door and set the timer for 15 minutes. This was the first time I had tried Sam´s process and random thoughts and connections were being made while I sat there and when the timer went off I felt more focused and clear. I decided to re-arrange the priority in what was deemed the most important.

To Fix	No:	Blockers	No:	Enablers	No:
Output	9	Parts not available at the right time	11	Golden rules for planning	11
Parts availability	8	Working capital tied up in WIP	9	No works order issued with shortages	10
Cost reduction	6	Mismatch of shifts and poor flow	7	Late customisation	6
Cash Flow	5	Too many production slots for build	7	Not enough sub assembly build	6
Process flow/design	5	Too much WIP	6	Poor performance metrics – visibility	6
Line balancing	5	No golden rules for planning	5	Production line simulation	5
Too much WIP	5	Too many "options" and complexity	5	Line balancing and process design	5
Too much choice /customisation	4	Identity of orders locked in too early	4	Reduce number of production slots	4
Too many unfinished orders	4	Shortages on works orders	3	Create buffer stocks with suppliers	3

Performance management	4	No visibility of cash tied up in WIP	3	Balance and match the shifts	3
Working capital reduction	3	Poor performance due to shortages	2	Better communication of results	2
Poor planning	3	Planning is impossible in this situation	1	Input from shop floor into process	2
Purchasing and planning not aligned	3	Poor relationship with suppliers	1	Creative problem solving methods	1
Totals	64		64		64

Using this list in this format I could see that Output was the most critical item in the first column so I put that down as the first thing to be fixed. I then changed the position of items like Too Much WIP that appeared in more than one column. I picked a single column for each repeating item, and added their numbers together. This gave me another re-jigged table that I will show you later.

As I looked at the list I began to see relationships that we could potentially exploit. For example if we were able to increase output there would be an automatic reduction in unit cost if nothing else changed. If we could do this by reducing the number of production slots then we would automatically reduce the amount of work in progress and this would in turn free up working capital for the business. I started to get excited at the possibilities I could see in front of me and I was itching to get back to Brian and Mal to tell them my thoughts.

I took a deep breath and sat back in my chair. I realised that I was getting way too far ahead of myself. I was already in solution mode when we had not even decided for sure what the one key problem was. I needed to get back to the guys and listen to what they had to say as well, to make sure that I was on the right track. I looked at my watch. It was almost 3pm, so I jumped up and headed off to Paul Howard's office.

As I got there Leon was just getting up from a chat with Paul. He smiled at me and said "Hi Ralph, you look all pumped up, have you been having a good day? Making progress?"

I couldn't believe my luck to get them both in the office at the same time. I said "I've had a great day Leon, and I was just about to sit with Paul and get some advice on which way we might be heading".

Leon smiled again and said "Well in that case, I will stick around for a few minutes and see what you have got. You don't mind?"

Of course I didn't mind – I could barely contain myself at this stroke of good luck. Although Leon was enthusiastic with everyone, his infectious personality made him feel like a definite ally to me, and having him around could only help in getting my troubled relationship with Paul Howard on the right track.

I laid my notes out on the meeting table and said "Brian, Mal, and I agreed this morning that we would go back to all of the key people today to get some consensus of where we're heading – we asked them these key questions," I said, handing them a copy of the list.

They both had a look and Paul said "What was your objective with this, Ralph?"

"We wanted to feed back what we had found to all of the key people and make sure we weren't missing anything. We also wanted to start to narrow down the focus so that we only concentrate on fixing one key thing – whatever seems like the most important element. We also wanted to flush out any potential blockers and enablers in advance. The guys helped me out a lot with this today, they have been very helpful".

Leon looked up and said "I can see what you are doing with this and it seems like a decent way to start. You're keeping people involved and in the loop and also making sure that you get down to the nub of the issue so that we can all move forward in agreement. I like this approach".

I could sense that Paul Howard was feeling left out of this conversation, and boss or no boss he was going to make his presence felt. "So what exactly is it that you need from me?" he snapped.

But his attitude was misplaced – there actually was something I wanted from him. I said "Paul, you are the most experienced vehicle builder in the whole business and you know this process inside out. There is something that I can't quite understand and I was hoping you could explain it to me".

This threw him for a moment. "Ah, OK, what do you need help with?"

"Well, let me try to describe what I am observing," I said, and pulled a pad of paper from my briefcase to scribble on.

I talked through the problems I had identified in regards to the production process, and wrote them down in bullet points for him. Paul looked at the list and asked "Okay, so what can we do to clarify the situation?"

I said "If this was a conventional vehicle plant there would be lots of automation and assembly lines or a continuous process of some kind and there would be no option to have vehicles with no parts available. It would simply not work. Here at Millikan we have a bespoke process instead, which is one of our big selling points and something our customers appreciate". Leon smiled at this. "We don't want to take anything away from that but I feel pretty sure that we could simulate an assembly line in some way, to get everyone in the factory working to the same drum beat. We also have WIP coming out of our ears which is swallowing loads of cash every day and bankrupting the company". Leon and Paul´s faces both twitched a little at the b-word, but I continued; "Now, I'm not a vehicle builder or a process designer, but I can see that this isn't working".

Paul had stared silently throughout this description. Despite their joint squirm when I had mentioned bankruptcy, the difference between Paul's face and Leon's was generally like comparing a thunderstorm to a bright spring day. I knew I had hit a raw nerve. "You want me to tell you how to do your job, maybe?" he snarled at me.

"Slow down Paul," said Leon in a soothing tone, "Ralph, what you seem to be saying is that you think we have watched this situation getting worse and worse and not done anything about it – is that right?

I was back pedalling madly in my mind, and suspected I'd made a big tactical error here. I said "Forgive me Leon, I may have put some of that a little clumsily. I guess what I am asking is, what are the early warning signs that the situation is getting out of control?"

"Ah, now that is a different question" said Leon as he looked at Paul. I think the best man to speak to might be Martin Kirkbride. He has all the numbers that you could ever want and he should be able to identify any key markers".

I said "I am going to see Martin tomorrow so I will ask him that. But I was trying to tease out something a little more practical. For example why do we keep building chassis when we know that the framing area is full of vehicles that are not moving fast enough?"

Paul Howard interjected "Well how else do we keep the guys on the shop floor busy?"

I said "If the guys were multi skilled and flexible as to where they could work, we could redeploy them when there is a glut in one area and a shortage in another. That way, you keep them busy and at the same time reduce your WIP and your working capital requirement".

"Ha, brilliant!" exclaimed Leon. "I love it! But is it really possible? It seems that something like that would be a great idea on paper, but I need you to think through the practicalities. If we can achieve what you are suggesting it would be a complete game changer. Hell, if you can do it, I'll give you a car!"

I was amazed at this. "I will remind you of your offer when we get this place buzzing!"

I then said to them both "I have done a spreadsheet exercise and it looks like the number one thing that needs to be fixed is output. Do you both agree with that?"

They looked at each other and Leon said "I would agree with that". Paul Howard nodded his grudging assent.

"Okay then, now we need to communicate that to all staff. There are a number of blockers and enablers which I have drawn up on this spreadsheet. I am going to sit down with Brian and Mal later to agree how to prioritise them and when we have done that I will send you both a copy".

Leon said "That sounds fine. Who is going to be doing the communicating?"

"I would like you to do it Leon. I think it is important that the initiative is seen to be backed at the highest level. That will give it the right level of importance from day one. I could prepare you some slides if it would help?"

"That would definitely help, I'd appreciate that. When should we tell the staff?" asked Leon

I replied "I think that we need to do it this week so that we can get into the meaty stuff next week and maintain momentum".

"Are you okay with that Paul?" said Leon.

Paul was still a bit hot under the collar and he said "I suppose so. I just hope it doesn't stir things up in the meantime".

I said "I fully agree Paul, and I hope you'll keep us on the right track while we are doing this".

Paul was still not happy to be an ally and grunted "Just run anything sensitive past me before you do it, okay?"

Leon Musket got up and said "I'll expect the slides tomorrow morning

Ralph. If we are doing it this week, I'll need to know what I'm saying as soon as possible".

"I'll get them to you by mid-morning tomorrow" I said

Leon left and I started to collect the papers off the table when Paul said in a low voice "If you embarrass me in front of Leon again I will walk you off the premises personally, bank or no bank".

I was shocked and I knew I had to build a bridge quickly. I said "Paul, you are absolutely right. I was clumsy and I should have known better. I will try to see to it that we are better aligned in future".

"Make sure that you do" said Paul, and picked up his phone.

That was the sign for me to exit, so I headed off to see Brian and Mal.

I found them both in Brian's office waiting for me. I was glad to be among friends again. I told them what had just happened with Leon and Paul. Brian looked thoughtful and said "Paul is a tough guy and you do not want to get on the wrong side of him, but he has his own opinions and there's not a lot you can do other than show him that there may be a better way. I am sure he will come around when he sees the progress we are making".

Mal said "Okay, enough of the negative stuff, what are we doing now?"

"We're going through my prioritised list to agree on the next step" I said. I laid the spreadsheet on the table and started to explain what I had done:

To Fix	No:	Blockers	No:	Enablers	No:
Output	9	Parts not available at the right time	37	Golden rules for planning	11
Cost reduction	6	Mismatch of shifts and poor flow	17	No works order issued with shortages	10
Cash Flow	5	Too much WIP	11	Late customisation	6
Performance management	4	No golden rules for planning	9	Not enough sub assembly build	6
Working capital reduction	3	Too many "options" and complexity	9	Poor performance metrics – visibility	6
Purchasing and planning not aligned	3	Too many production slots for build	7	Production line simulation	5
		Identity of orders locked in too early	4	Line balancing and process design	5
		No visibility of cash tied up in WIP	3	Reduce number of production slots	4
		Poor relationship with suppliers	1	Create buffer stocks with suppliers	3
				Balance and match the shifts	3
				Better communication of results	2
				Input from shop floor into process	2
				Creative problem solving methods	1
Totals	30		98		64

To get the PDF template for the Blockers and Enablers Worksheet and video tutorial go to: **www.90daystoprofit.co.uk/bonus**

"I am convinced that output is the number one thing that we need to tackle, so it's at the top of the list in column one. The other things in column one still need to be tackled so I have left them there for later. I have consolidated the comments from column one and two when I thought we were really saying the same thing in different words. I have added the scores together when I have done the consolidation and reprioritised the list from high to low. You can see from the list that parts availability is the number one blocker that we need to tackle. Again, there are lots of other blockers which I have left in place to tackle later. The last column is the enablers and I have left that column in place but just prioritised it from high to low and it looks like planning is the thing that will help us most in our task".

Mal said "I think that all of this is connected. We cannot do any of it in isolation and when we unlock the puzzle and start to make improvements we will surely get benefits in lots of different areas of the business".

I was delighted with this insight, and said "I am with you on that one, Mal. For example we might find that we need to rebalance the shifts and reduce the number of production slots when we get into this properly. That in turn might make planning easier, align the processes, reduce the WIP and also free up working capital for the business. You are right, these things are all connected so we need to be mindful that whatever we change will have an effect somewhere else and make sure that we are not making one thing better and at the same time making something else worse".

We all agreed with this. "Great," I said, "so can you guys help me set up the communications sessions later in the week?"

"Sure we can" said Brian. "I think we should also check out your slides before you give them to Leon to make sure that there is nothing sensitive in there".

"I am happy for you to do that Brian, I've stepped on enough land mines for one week!"

Getting the Message Out

Next morning I was in my office early and I started creating the slides on my laptop for Leon. I started with a simple outline for what the slides would say:

Ralph is here to help us. He is sponsored by the bank and he is here to take the business forward. He is using a structured step by step process to understand what is happening in the business. He is getting input from every part of the business and welcomes your views at any time. He has the full support of the senior management team. Ralph along with Brian and Mal have been observing the process and interviewing people over the last week. We are now all in agreement that the one thing that needs to be improved in the business is output. Over the next week these same guys along with others will start to collect data and information about the subject of output. They will seek input from every level of the business and find out everything they can about output and what affects it. They will dig deep where they have to, they will seek opinions, and they will interrogate all of the available metrics. They will share their findings with the senior team and all key people in the business to keep everyone on the same page. Please give them your full support and cooperation this week and if you have any suggestions please give them to the guys as they come round.

From this storyboard I created a simple set of slides slide with that message on it in a little more detail, thinking about it as if I was speaking to the audience myself. I also decided to have only one point per slide to avoid death by PowerPoint.

I thought that this was a fairly succinct message and I decided to share the presentation with Brian. I was about to head out towards his office when, coincidentally, he stuck his head into mine.

"Hi Brian, come in and have a look at what I have done so far" I said.

I took Brian through the story board first which was very quick and then we went through the slides one by one and explained what each slide was meant to be doing for the audience. It only took 20 minutes which was great timing for this sort of communication. Any longer than that and people start to lose concentration.

Brian had been making notes as he was going through and said "Well, overall, it's a good presentation. But can we really say that we have the full support of the senior team? Even Paul Howard? What I would ask Leon to say is that the team doing this work has his full support, which I believe is true".

I was making notes as Brian was talking. "That is good advice Brian. Is there anything else?"

"Brian replied "Well it is clear that we have not spoken to all of the people in all departments of the company because there are simply too many of them, so it might be wise to emphasise the offer to everyone that if they want to speak to any of the team this week then they can come and see us if they have permission from their line manager".

"That sounds good. I want to make sure that we uncover every nugget of information that we can find".

"Yes, we don't have all of the answers, and the people out there doing it every day will have lots of insights that will help us. Being able to come and talk to us should also help people get enthusiastic about this process – they'll feel more of a sense of ownership".

I knew I had a real gem in Brian and I was truly fired up by his commitment to this cause.

"So what do you think we should do about the timing and arrangements for the communications?" I asked.

"Leave that to me. There are lots of departments here and we're all on different shifts, so I will need to work out the best times to catch everyone. Leon is very flexible and he will come in at midnight if needs be to make sure everyone gets the same message directly from him".

"Great, I'll modify the slides a little and then go and speak to Leon about the presentation. I'll tell him that you're working out the timings for him, is that okay?"

"Sure thing, I'll get right on it and come back to you later today. Just so you know, we have a communications specialist in HR who normally helps with this sort of thing. I will introduce you to her later. Shoot me and Mal a copy of your slides when you are done".

I was beginning to understand just how important communications were in this new role. The changes that Brian had suggested were not immediately obvious to me, but I knew that they were an improvement on what we had started with and I also knew that we now had a better chance of success because of it. I was learning more and more every day.

I got the slides into good shape and arranged to meet Leon in an hour to discuss them. I also sent a copy of the slides and storyboard to Brian and Mal.

When I arrived at Leon's office he was just finishing up with a visitor and I was surprised to see that it was Simon Brown, the bank manager who had brought me into Millikan. Simon smiled and said "Hello Ralph, Leon tells me you are already making good progress"

I returned the smile and said "Hello Simon. It is nice to know that I am getting a good report already".

"Well, we could both see something in you that we liked. We know you will give it 100% and more. Good luck this week".

Simon left the office and I looked at Leon. Was it bad news that the bank manager was visiting? On the contrary, it seemed. "Simon and I go way back," said Leon, "he has always supported us and he really wants us to get through this bad patch and get things buzzing. So he and I will support you in every way we can to achieve it. I am not a manufacturing expert after all, I'm an inventor! Come and have a walk with me Ralph and tell me what you have got for me. I like to do walking meetings whenever I can". With that he grabbed his safety gear and started heading for the factory. He said "I always like to get around the shop floor at least once a day to see for myself what is going on and to let the guys know that I am interested in them. Now tell me what you have got".

I pulled out the printout and showed Leon the slides. I explained that I had gone through things in detail with Brian this morning.

"I thought that might be the case. Brian knows how I like to communicate so I am pleased that he has helped you with this process" said Leon, who seemed to be an expert at walking and reading at the same time – I guess practice makes perfect.

I said "So should we go through the slides in detail?"

"No need" said Leon. "I read through the brief that you sent me and it all looks good. I will edit the slides later today to get them into my 'voice' and then we should be all set".

"That's great Leon. I will speak to Brian about the timing for the communications sessions and get back to you".

"Sounds like a plan to me Ralph, thanks for that".

By this time we were in the middle of the assembly shop and one of the supervisors was calling to Leon so it was my cue to exit. Back in my office I decided to get in a 15 minute session of thinking time and reflect on everything that had happened over the last few days. It hardly seemed credible that I had come so far and learned so much in that short time.

I was starting to see that it was not enough to just have a step-by-step process of the kind that Sam was teaching me. Inside every major step there were a number of sub-steps and these would vary with the type of business and the type of problem to be fixed. Also each sub-step required skills to be applied expertly to get the best possible result. And underlying this were the people skills and the social land mines that I had already managed to step on a couple of times in my first week at Millikan. I was starting to see that the really good business consultants and interim managers were very skilled people who had learned their craft over a period of time and had probably learned by making some pretty fundamental mistakes along the way. I vowed at that moment to do whatever it would take to be the best transformation specialist that I could be. If I needed to be coached or get additional training then I would do it. I wanted to get fantastic results for my clients and make this a lifelong career that I could be proud of. I also wanted to make a good life for Maricel and I could see that this was a way for me to do that. I was thinking that due to my working background I might be better suited to doing interim management work where I could go into a business and take on a senior role where I was a part of the management team charged with achieving a particular result in a given time frame. But that was getting ahead of myself. I would look into that possibility for my next assignment. In the meantime, I was here to do a great job for Millikan.

When the countdown timer chimed after 15 minutes, I wrote down my notes and walked over to see Brian. He was in his office and talking on the phone as I came in. Brian nodded and motioned for me to sit down. When he had finished on the phone he said "That was Laura, our communications specialist. We were discussing how to get the sessions done this week. We have decided to do the first one for all office staff in the main assembly hall tomorrow morning from 10 to 10:30. We have held lots of comms sessions there before and Laura knows how to get it set up with screens and microphones and so on. She is going to get that done now. The second session will be at 1:45pm and the last session will be at 9:45pm. For those sessions each set of shift workers will either finish fifteen minutes early and stay fifteen minutes late; or come in fifteen minutes early and start work fifteen minutes after their scheduled time. In all those cases we will have to pay 15 minutes overtime to everyone who is hourly paid which is a cost to the business and also we will lose 60 minutes of total production across the whole site, so this is a significant investment and we need to ensure we get this communication right".

I had not considered this before. With over 1000 people on the shop floor at an average salary of £30,000 I was asking the business for a substantial investment in putting this message out for everyone. On top of that was one full hour of lost production in every department. I would not underestimate the cost or the value of communications again.

Brian continued "I am assuming that you will be attending all of the sessions along with Leon, Mal, and myself?"

I had not thought about that but I said yes straightaway. I asked "How does this normally work Brian?"

"Well this is not a normal session for us but I am guessing that Leon would like you, me, and Mal to be alongside him at the front of the room to show support and to answer any questions at the end. If he is working 15 hours in the day to get this done he'll expect us to do the same".

"Well if that is the case then you can count on me. I will be there to do my bit alongside Leon and you guys".

"Great, we have to show a united front to get across the visual message that we are all behind this initiative. The words are fine but the visual message is also very strong".

I had not considered that either. I sure was learning a lot today. I was starting to feel a little out of my depth again. I was definitely going to have a lot to discuss with Sam next time I saw him.

Brian said "Come on, I will show you where we're doing the presentations so that you are familiar with the area and you know what to expect".

We both grabbed our safety gear and headed off into the factory. At one end of the assembly hall there was a large open area where they parked the vehicles prior to final test. They could park the vehicles around the outside of this area and create a very large open space. On the end wall there was a huge drop down screen that could be used for presentations, with a high powered projector in the rafters. There was a portable stage to one side of the screen with a lectern and microphone stand. There was also a transparent autocue system set up so that the speaker could look at his notes and at the audience at the same time. It was slick. They had thought about how to do this properly.

I got myself familiar with the area and Brian pointed out where we would be standing when Leon gave his presentation. Brian also said that there would be assistants from the HR department with wifi microphones to hand to us and to anyone who wanted to ask a question. They had thought of everything it seemed. Brian showed me an area to one side which had a small table and a pile of question forms. He said "Some people don't like to ask questions in front of an audience so this allows them to get their question considered without speaking up in front of everyone in the business".

I headed home that night and made sure to relax and mentally prepare myself for the next day. I was looking forward to these communication sessions, but still a little anxious due to my lack of experience. Nothing a good night's sleep wouldn't fix, or at least that's what I tried to convince myself.

At 9:45 the next day Brian came to my office and said "Come on Ralph, time to put on a show".

I was ready. I had printed off a bunch of notes just in case I was asked any difficult questions. I was keen to get down there and take part in the event.

When we got to the assembly area the office staff were starting to arrive. There were no seats, it was an all-standing affair to encourage us to keep the presentation short and sweet – 30 minutes was long enough to stand in one spot.

At 9:55 Leon arrived and took his place on the lectern. Myself, Brian and Mal were off to his right at the lower level and Laura from Comms was at the back of the room, shepherding people into position. The HR assistants were standing by with microphones in hand. It was all set. Leon looked at me and winked.

Bang on 10am Leon brought the meeting to order and he began his performance. I watched as he went through the presentation and noted his style. He was very confident in his delivery and he came across very well. He used pauses to emphasise certain points and he looked around the area to make eye contact with as many people as possible. I remembered how important it was to be a great presenter.

At the end of the slides Leon asked for questions. Tommy Sherwin raised his hand and he was soon handed a microphone. He looked around the room and then said "Leon, thank you for your presentation and bringing us all up to date with what is happening. I would just like to check that when we are talking about improving output we are not talking about making my members work longer hours than they currently are. These guys are already working hard under very difficult circumstances".

Leon was clearly expecting this question as he answered immediately "Tommy, thank you so much for your question. I can understand why you would have that concern. We will not change anything until all of us are agreed on what it is that we are changing and what that entails to everyone involved. As a business we cannot carry on the way that we are doing now. That much is clear. We have identified that output is the one thing that we are going to fix. The next steps are for the team" (he nodded at me and the other two guys) "to gather as much detail and insight as we possibly can over the next week or so to give us the information that we need to create the next step in the process. And I'll be looking forward to seeing your input into this data-gathering step so that we can properly and accurately reflect the needs of your members in this process. I would not have it any other way".

Tommy looked around thoughtfully and then said "Thank you Leon I will make sure that I give the team the benefit of my experience" and there was a quiet ripple of laughter around the area.

Leon smiled and said "Thanks Tommy. Any further questions?"

There did not seem to be any more takers so Leon said "Okay, that's fine. If any of you think of a question after the session there are question forms on the side table down here. Just grab a form, fill in your question and hand it to your line manager, anyone in HR, or any of the team here. Thank you everyone".

Leon got down off the lectern and came over to see me, Brian and Mal. He said "I think that went pretty well, guys?" We nodded our assent. "But don't forget that this is the staff group. These people are usually pretty quiet and reserved. We may get a different response from the other groups. See you at 13:45, same place". With that he walked off back in the direction of his office.

The place started to empty and people were chatting among themselves. I walked through the crowd and picked up on the conversations that were taking place and I was relieved to hear that the reaction to the presentation for the most part was positive. This had definitely got off to a good start.

The other sessions during the day all went off well. Leon did his piece very well as expected. There were a lot more questions from the audience and myself and Brian were called on to answer some of them. We did so with ease as we were intimately involved with the process and the material. By 10:30pm I was pleased that we had got through the day in one piece with no major obstacles to overcome. I knew that we were on the right track and I also now knew that we had the backing of the key players in the business and most of the staff.

Next week it was time to start gathering the data and I was really looking forward to that. By the time I got home that night it was 11pm and I was still buzzing from the progress we had made. When I pulled into the drive I noticed that the house was dark again and I had the same sinking feeling. I could not believe how stupid and insensitive I had become just lately. When I had turned up late after my first day of work I had promised Maricel that I would make it up to her tonight by going out for an old-fashioned date, and I had blown it again. What the hell was going on in my mind this week? My head was so full of my new assignment that I was forgetting to work at keeping my marriage together. It had been a rough few months while I had been out of work, and Maricel had supported us with her salary which had been a struggle. I was repaying her by forgetting she existed. I opened the front door and stepped into the dark hallway. I turned on the light and shouted "Hi honey", but I knew there would be no answer. The house was completely silent. There was no Maricel. There was another note on the side table in the hall and it said "Ralph, I have gone to stay with my mother for a few days. You are clearly not thinking about me or our marriage. I will call you when I have got my mind into a better place, Maricel". Just when things seemed to be looking up at work, I now had a crisis in my marriage. I poured myself a drink.

P IS FOR PROBLEMS:
RALPH'S REFLECTIONS

When I started work again I had promised myself that I would sit down with a notebook each week to capture what I had learned. I got up on Saturday morning, grabbed my journal and started writing some notes, not just about what Sam was teaching me but also about my life.

In week one I had learned that the first thing you must do is to identify the one thing that the business needs to fix. You cannot get ahead of yourself and try to solve every little issue that you find. It is vital to speak to as many key people as possible to get a good cross section of opinions about what needs to be fixed. In this way you do not get led down the wrong path too early in the process. It is important to create the informal team or teams very early in the process because it is impossible to do all of this by yourself. Also the team members have lots of expert job knowledge that they can bring to you – avoiding the need for you to learn a lot of stuff before anything can be done. You can use the skills and experience of the team to validate your information and observations in this first step, so that you can move forward with a solid foundation in place.

Once the team has identified the one thing that needs to be fixed the CEO or site leader must also agree so that the process can move forward. Once this agreement is secured, the CEO should then lead the site wide communications so that it has the necessary weight and gravitas very early and every person in the business can understand the importance of what needs to be done. The team must agree on the message that will be communicated through the business, so that the CEO can get the right message across without any misunderstanding. It is also important that the CEO uses their own style to deliver the message, as it must come across as being authentic.

In the actual communication sessions you must ask for the support of the people who are receiving the message. They need to know that their input and contribution is important and that they will be listened to. Part of the message must be that the project is achievable and that there is a structured way of getting it done.

If there are any non-negotiable issues such as product quality, those things must be front of mind in whatever is done next so that there are no conflicts further into the process.

I had learnt that walking meetings were a valid and useful option to discuss issues in a time efficient way and I could see myself using them more often. I had educated myself on how I could increase my energy levels by eating alkaline foods and starting the day with a green smoothie. 15 minutes thinking time had also proven an effective way of coming up with great solutions and clearing my head during the work day.

Paul Howard was testing my resolve but he had taught me an important lesson about my own expertise in the area of people skills, and I was determined to improve my skills and win him over if it was the last thing that I did.

Personal Life

In terms of my personal problems I had identified several and I had finally admitted to myself that I was totally unfit and carrying too much weight and I had to do something about that starting now. I was also getting too deeply involved in the business at the expense of my relationship with Maricel and that had to change quickly

Work/life balance was not something I had been concerned about before but it was pretty high on my list now and I was convinced that I had to start putting more effort into my relationship with Maricel.

I was beginning to understand how much I did not know about life and about management and that was a sobering experience in many ways. I promised myself that I would become a lifelong student from now on and learn something new and valuable every day. I was beginning to realise that there was a lot more to management and consultancy than just technical skills and knowledge

From a personal standpoint it had been a difficult week. I had forgotten about a celebratory dinner I had promised Maricel, and then stood her up on our date. I was also beginning to realise just how out of shape I was. Dashing around the factory and up and down the office stairs was taking its toll on me. At least I had cut down a little on my drinking – not completely, and I fell off the wagon quite sharply when things went badly with Maricel, but I was making some progress. I was wondering, however, if I had made the right career choice if it was going to have such a negative impact on my marriage.

> To get the free in depth video tutorial on this step of
> 7 Steps to Profit go to **www.90daystoprofit.co.uk/bonus**

7 STEPS TO PROFIT

2 Review

1 Problems

CHAPTER TWO

R IS FOR REVIEW

SAM'S SESSION 2

I turned up 20 minutes early at the session next morning. I was like an excited puppy, eager to tell Sam how my first week had gone. Sam listened intently, and seemed pleased with how things were going, but he warned me "Don't get ahead of yourself Ralph. You have already spotted lots of opportunities, which is quite common. The key to step 1, however, is that you cannot move forward until everyone is on board. That means from the top to the bottom and everyone in between. It doesn't matter what the thing is that you're going to fix, as long as everyone agrees that it is the right thing to do at this time". I could have carried on talking about turning this company around for hours, but the rest of the group had started to trickle in, and it was time to get the second session underway.

Sam launched into the session straight away. "Right guys, tell me what you have achieved in week 1, I want to make sure that you're making good progress". After a good discussion of early difficulties and teething problems that we were having, Sam recapped the first step.

"Remember, step one is to narrow down the focus and agree what it is that you are going to fix. You should have created an informal team or teams, and you should be getting sign-off and full agreement from the top of the business and communicating this to all staff before you move forward. You need to go round the key people in the business multiple times to get everyone in the loop and make sure everyone has had their say and you have a clear direction. Do not attempt to take things forward before you have got all of this in place. It's tempting to see something that you can fix straight away and get stuck in. Next thing you know, that one thing has turned into two things and then three things and before you know it you have been there for 6 months and you have made a few small improvements but not even made a dent in the real thing that needs to be fixed. Do not fall into that trap. So are we all ready for step 2?"

Sam went to the board and said "Okay guys you know the drill. What is step 2? What does R stand for?"

We started to fire suggestions. Sam captured them on the board as we went along without making any comment. After a few minutes the ideas slowed to a trickle and Sam said "Okay guys, it looks like we have some good suggestions of where to go next, but let me make it easier for you. The next step after deciding what to fix is to gather all of the information that you possibly can about that thing. The second part is to analyse the information that you have gathered, and you can do both of these things at the same time which is why I have amalgamated these two steps into one. I used to keep them separate, but as I became more experienced at using this methodology it made sense to do them together. You need to become the resident expert on your particular subject. For example, in Ralph's case it looks like output is the thing that we need to fix. In the next week I fully expect that Ralph and his team will gather every bit of data that they can about output and what makes it go up and down, what are the levers that you need to pull, what will allow it to increase, what are the resource implications, how process flow and supervision affect output, and 20 other things that I haven't even thought of yet. They will analyse all of this data and really understand what they need to do in that business to make a positive impact on output".

He said "Once you have been given your mission and you have determined exactly what problem you need to address then you need to understand everything that you can about that problem given the current conditions and time frame. Following on from my first example last week we were given the task of rescuing a high ranking general who had been captured by the enemy. We had no idea who was holding him, where he was being held, if he was still alive, what obstacles we had to overcome, what equipment or skills we would need or anything else about the situation. In this step you would gather all of the information that you could in the time frame allowed. You would maybe scout the area, gather intelligence from other units, look in detail at the terrain or the topography of the area, identify any ambush points or fall back positions and a host of other things to improve your knowledge of the situation. Once you had done all of this you would get your best people around the table and look at all of the intelligence and information to agree exactly what you were facing before you committed any of your time or resources into the mission. You want to give yourself the best chance of success. It is exactly the same in a business context – although usually you are not in a life and death situation".

I was scribbling quickly to capture what Sam was saying because I knew that his comments were intended to help me specifically.

Sam then went on to tell us how to analyse the data. He had a particular way of doing it which was reliant on having decent numbers going back at least 3 years. His view was that there was always value in looking at the messages of the past. Sometimes companies forget what they already know. He would plot out all of the relevant data over the longest time frame available and identify any trends and connections. For example he might look at turnover and headcount together; he might look at number of orders quoted against number of orders won. It all depended on the situation he found himself in.

Ideally, all of this data can then be portrayed on a trend graph over the same time frame, creating a storyboard to tease out the messages that were hidden in plain sight the whole time. Seeing things visually by using graph frameworks is a great way to get our mind thinking more clearly about a solution, as well as making things easy for other team members to grasp.

The targets for the same time frame should also be graphically shown so that they can be compared to performance. All companies base their projections on a budget of some kind. The budget is based on a set of assumptions that have targets baked into them. If the targets are not being met or exceeded then the budget will not be adhered to and profit will not be achieved.

When I listened to Sam describing all of this it became clear that he knew what he was talking about and that he had done it many times before.

I was starting to think that I would never reach Sam's level but then I gave myself a mental slap. My focus at this stage was to learn my craft and get a great result for Millikan – the naval gazing could come later.

The insight I gained from this session was that most managers never do this stuff. They look at the results for their division or department, and check whether it's going up or down, close to target or not. But they really didn't do much with the data or the messages that were right in front of their faces. They also did not do the trend comparisons that we had done that morning. Sam turned to me: "So Ralph, you have a good idea what to do with your data this week. What do you think you are going to find?"

"I think that I am going to find that this business has not been hitting its own targets for a long time. I think that the output will be too variable and way below the required level. I think that the headcount will have been rising with no corresponding rise in output. I also think that the WIP will have been growing to the point where it is eating most of the cash in the business and very little has been done about it. Apart from that, I think things will look great!" Everyone had a laugh at this last bit. Sam was also smiling; he said "You're learning quickly Ralph. I will be keen to hear how you get on this week so be prepared to give us a detailed brief next time".

Sam was in my corner and giving me good feedback and guidance. I was hoping for a good week ahead.

We spent the rest of the session discussing how we would collect and analyse the data and how we would capture all of the contributing factors around the subject to make a meaningful contribution to our businesses. At the end of the session we were all buzzing and keen to get out and put our knowledge to work on our projects.

Sam called me over before leaving and said "You are doing really well Ralph, I think you have a natural talent for this kind of work. If you need any help just give me a call. But do think about how to deal with Paul Howard. He is number two in the company, and it's critical to the success of this project that you get him on your side. It is no good having allies lower down the organisation if you do not have the full backing of the senior team".

I smiled and thanked Sam for his help. I still didn't feel totally confident in my new role, and I was worried I'd be found out as an imposter with no idea what I was doing, but it made all the difference to have Sam backing me so I left the session with a spring in my step, ready to face the new week at Millikan.

Gathering and Analysing Data

The following Monday I got into work feeling fresh and energised, as I had been eating alkaline foods and cutting down a little on the beer. I started my day by making a list of all the people who could possibly help me with the data gathering step. The first name on my list was Martin Kirkbride, the CFO. He had told me to come and see him if I wanted any metrics or numbers for any part of the business, so I gave him a call to see if he was at work yet. He answered on the first ring "Good morning Ralph, I was expecting your call" said Martin.

"Good morning, Martin. I did think you might be expecting a call from me after the presentations on Friday" I replied. "Are you free sometime today?"

"Come over right now if you are ready to start" said Martin.

I grabbed my notes folder and set off for Martin's office. As I was walking along the corridor I was pleasantly surprised to see that lots of people were in early. The official start to the day for office staff was 08:30 but it was only 07:45 and already many people were at work. I like to see that. It tells me that they enjoy coming to work, they are keen and want to come in early and get cracking.

Martin's door was open so I tapped on the door frame and went in. Martin was on the phone and he motioned for me to sit. As I was waiting for him to finish I took a look at the pictures of his wife and children in the office, along with some great photos of old cars. A good family man, as well as a car nut. A lot of people here were car nuts.

He put down the phone and said "Right, let's get to it Ralph. What can I tell you?"

"Well, you know we have communicated that we are going to focus on output as our priority. What do we have in terms of data regarding output?" I responded.

"We have a ton of data about output but just let me put it into context first. There are eight manufacturing departments here, and they all have different ways of measuring what they do. Some of them are multi-dimensional, like the body shop that measures front ends, rear ends, side frames, floors and roofs. Then they measure the total number of bodies delivered to the paint shop. As another example we have chassis build and they measure their output in target fabrication hours versus actual fabrication hours. I normalise their output into FVE which stands for Finished Vehicle Equivalents – but you won't find that anywhere except on my database".

I had a dawning realisation that this was going to take longer than I had expected.

"So out of all the departments how many of them can we measure in terms of FVE's?" I asked.

"With a bit of work we can get them all to do it, but at the moment half of them are sort of there and the other half are not".

"So how do I go about understanding how they set their targets and how they measure their performance or their output?" I wondered.

"I guess the best place to start is with me, because I can give you my version of what the numbers look like, based on the assumptions I have built into the database. That will be a good grounding for you. Then I would suggest that you talk to the planners for each area and see how they do it" said Martin.

That seemed like a good suggestion to me "How long would it take for you to give me the output data that you have by department and for the entire factory?"

Martin stroked his chin and said "Better than that, I can give you full access to the data so that you can interrogate it yourself, but I will have to give you a tutorial on how to get at it and how to interpret it. That will take about 2 hours I should think. I could do it this afternoon straight after lunch if that suits you?"

"That will be fine for me" I said "I will go and have a preliminary word with the planners in the meantime".

"Sounds good," said Martin, "bring a big notepad".

When I had finished with Martin I made my way down to see Brian. He and I were becoming joined at the hip, and he was a great help to me. He was not in his office so I made my way over to Mal's and found them both in there looking at a screen.

Brian looked sombre, and said: "Have you seen the news?". He was pointing at the screen. Millikan was featured on the 24 hour BBC news channel, with the headline saying '1400 jobs on the line at Millikan Automotive'. The sub-header: '60 days of cash left in the business before the company is bankrupt'. Leon had been filmed reading a statement to camera insisting that all jobs in the company would be safe as long as he was in charge, and stating that a process was already underway to fix some of systemic issues that had put Millikan in this position. His face was serious, but his tone of voice was comforting at the same time as being authoritative. I hopes it would be enough to keep the factory workers calm for now.

Mal said "Everyone in the business is talking about it and people are worried about their jobs". I was wondering how this had leaked, and I had a sinking feeling in my stomach. But I gave myself a shake of the head and realised there was no point reflecting on the doom and gloom all day – I had to get down to work and make sure that what

Leon was saying on that news story turned out to be true.

Brian said "So, you have been data gathering?" and sat down next to me.

"Yes indeed" I said. "I have just been with Martin Kirkbride and he has promised to give me access to all of the output data for the last 3 years from his accounting system".

Mal chipped in "That is a great start. Martin has tons of data which will be very useful. Did he make any other suggestions?"

"Yes, he suggested that I talk to the planners for each area to get their take on it" I replied.

"Also a great idea. Those guys will give it to you as straight as you like. They are a good bunch in the main" said Mal.

"I was hoping you could give me some names and locations so that I can start doing the rounds before I get back to Martin"

"No problem" said Brian and he started to write a list of names and office locations for me. There were 12 names on the list. I had not realised that there were so many planners here, but it was a large and complex business so maybe it shouldn't have been a surprise.

Brian said "This is the list of planners. They all report to a chief planner called Robert Cullen who sits in the office across from Paul Howard. He is a good guy, so go and speak to him first and let him know that you would like to speak to his team. Best to start out on the right foot".

That was Brian looking out for me again. This guy was a very skilled communicator.

"That sounds great. So how can you guys help me with this?"

"We can dig out all of the production data from the last 3 years, which will give you the numbers that each area has declared into the morning meeting. It may or may not be the same as the planners or the accounts numbers, but it is what we work on each day and each month for our reporting purposes".

"That sounds like a good idea" I said. "How about getting insights into the process and what affects output?"

Brian looked at me patiently "One thing at a time Ralph, let's make a start on the data and then we can look at the other stuff".

"Touché Brian – you sound just like me!" I laughed.

I headed off to see Robert and the other guys went off to gather their production data. Robert was very helpful, and gave me some useful data and opinions as to what he thought might be happening. I was getting used to taking notes very quickly and I filled a couple of sides of A4 in no time. He told me that when the business first started they had very few orders and they treated every vehicle like a mini project. As the company grew they simply expanded on that philosophy rather than change to something that was more in line with a mass production facility. This had its limitations and there were discussions going on in the business to look at different types of Enterprise Resource Planning systems, or ERP as it´s called, but for the moment they had what they had. Also the identity of each vehicle was locked in from the moment that the works order is launched. This could be problematic and had been discussed many times, but as yet no alternatives had been identified.

Ideally when the works order is raised, all materials and parts for that vehicle should be available in stock. As it stood currently, the materials for each vehicle were not always in stock at the plant before the works order is launched. That meant that they were always relying on materials arriving as the vehicle moves through the process. The early parts of the process such as body making were virtually identical, but even at that stage each car had a unique identity. There were excess, or buffer, stocks between some of the processes, but they did not seem to work as they should. There was an options list a mile long and each vehicle had a different specification. The wiring harness for each vehicle was different depending on the option list. All of this made the process tricky, hard to manage, and longer than was necessary.

They were gradually making things more standard as they were going along but it was taking a long time – and time was one commodity that they did not have. The process from end-to-end was not balanced. Inputs and outputs were variable and the shifts did not match. This led to build up of WIP in parts of the process, and shortages everywhere. When there was a shortage – which was every day – they parked up the vehicle with the shortage and moved to the next one which had parts available. All this did was create WIP and not finished goods, and it seemed to be a vicious cycle that was proving very hard to break out of. There was no official means to manage and monitor WIP. It was up to each area supervisor to manage their own WIP in their own preferred way.

A lot of time was spent running around looking for parts and there was no proper process to let production know when the parts had arrived. So this meant that the parts may have been available for days but they were not delivered to the line where they were badly needed. As a result of all of this the plan was hardly ever achieved on any shift in any department on any day. They had been running like this for over two years with no apparent improvement and Robert was of the view that if each car was more standard and was configured later in the process then this would unlock lots of potential output – I agreed.

It was a great starting point and Robert said it was fine for me to go round all of his guys and talk to them about the target versus actual performance from a planning perspective in each area. He said that he would send round a note quickly to let them all know.

I thanked him for his help and set off to meet my first area planner.

By lunch time I had seen 5 out of the 12 planners and made a ton of notes about the characteristics of the output in their areas. I was really learning a lot about the process and how it worked. In a short time I would probably be the most knowledgeable person in the whole business with regard to the overall process – just as Sam had recommended.

I made my way back to grab a quick bite of lunch, then I headed back to see Martin. He was waiting for me to arrive and said "I have set up a log in for you. You'll have to create your own password".

"Thanks Martin, how do you want to play this?"

"Let me start by giving you some background to the system and then I can show you everything you need".

For the next two hours I got to learn the accounts system inside out. I was not able to see the financial results for the business, just the raw data which was perfect for my needs. Martin was a very good teacher and once again I made a ton of notes.

At the end of it all I had to say "Enough Martin, my head is going to explode!"

He laughed and said "Welcome to my world Ralph, I get to wade through this treacle every day!"

We both laughed. I said "Rather you than me. If you don't mind I will write up my notes and have a go at sifting through the system to see if I can get the hang of it. After that, I'd probably like to come back and ask you some questions, if that's okay?"

"Sure Ralph, that'll be fine".

So I grabbed my notes and headed back to my office. As I reached the door I could hear the phone ringing. I stepped inside and picked up. It was Mal Davies. He said "How is it going Ralph? Have you got your head full of data by now?"

I said "You got it Mal. My head is so full of new stuff that I am going to have to let some of the old out!"

"Life was not meant to be easy Ralph. Anyway we have some more data for you down here when you are ready, you lucky man".

"Okay Mal, I will come down and get it now before I start to write up my notes".

In Mal's office there was a ton of printed papers in lots of different piles.

He said "We have been busy this morning. We've recovered all of the output data as declared in the morning meetings for the last 3 years. It is separated into each area, and it's in date order from newest to oldest. We have also collated all of this on to a spread sheet which I will send you by email so that you can play with the data and identify any trends".

I looked at the mountain of papers on the table and felt a bit overwhelmed. But these guys had pulled out all the stops today and I was really grateful.

"Thank you Mal, this will be a great help".

"No worries Ralph, glad to help".

I put all of the piles into order and set off back to my office with them.

When I got there I started to collate everything that we had gathered so far. I still had the other 7 planners to go and see but that would have to wait until tomorrow. I also had to interrogate the accounts system and dredge as much out of that as I could manage. It was going to be a busy week.

At home that night I was relieved to see that Maricel was back, but she was clearly not in a good mood. I decided to play it softly. I gave her a little peck on the cheek and said "How are you sweetheart? Did you have a good day?"

It didn't work. Straight away she said "Ralph, we cannot manage like this. We have got bills coming out of our ears and no money. What are you going to do about it? And I haven't forgiven you for standing me, up so don't get cocky".

So much for the small talk. "Okay honey, I know that I have some bridge building to do. I'll call the bank tomorrow. I will explain about the new contract that I am working on, let them know that I'll be getting a big chunk of cash in six weeks, and ask them to extend the overdraft until then".

"You had better do something Ralph, because I am getting final reminders every day now and it is getting too much to handle". She started to cry and that broke me up. I gave her a hug and told her that I would take care of it and that everything would be okay in a few weeks. She was still not convinced. She said "I can't live like this, Ralph. It needs to get better real soon or I really will go back to live with my parents. Don't act surprised Ralph," she said, seeing my reaction, "this has been coming for months. I can only take so much and I am reaching the end of my tether".

"Bear with me honey. It will be fine in a few weeks, I promise".

She grabbed her bag and said "I am going to see my friend Marge. You can get your own dinner".

With that she walked out and slammed the door.

This was all I needed. Things were going really well at work but to get this when I came home was not what I had in mind. I really wanted to get our marriage back on the tracks. We had been together for 6 years and things were going really well until this last year. I was determined to sort things out. In the meantime I just needed a few beers to settle my nerves. But then I thought about my promise to myself. I struggled with my demons briefly and then opted for a cup of tea instead, saying to myself: "If you wait till tomorrow, you can have two beers". I took this as a small triumph because any other time it would have been the whole six pack for sure.

Maricel came in after I had gone to bed and was sleeping in the spare room when I got up in the morning. I decided to leave her be and went to work early as usual.

When I got to my office I started to interrogate the accounts system that Martin had showed me yesterday. It was tricky to understand at first but after an hour or so I was making it sing. I started to collate the output data that I needed onto one giant spreadsheet so that I could play with the numbers as Mal Davies had suggested. It was all going rather well I thought.

I was keen to stay on this one task and not to get ahead of myself – this step in the process is all about data gathering and making sure that you are finding out as much as possible about the thing that needs fixing. The analysis would start later. For now I just had to make sure that I collected as much data about output that I possibly could. After lunch I made my rounds to see the other planners. This was all going well and I planned to sit down with Mal and Brian tomorrow to do a roundup of where we had got to.

The next morning I collated my notes and headed down to see Brian and Mal. They were both in the morning meeting so I slipped in discreetly and observed the proceedings. All of the area supervisors were present and they were just going through the output numbers as I arrived. They had a huge printed whiteboard on one wall and all of the departments were listed across the top. The days of the week were listed down the left hand side and some of them were split into shifts. All of the numbers had been hand written and they were colour coded red and green. Each supervisor was giving a very brief rundown of the previous day's results and any issues. There was a guy next to Brian taking notes and I could see that there was another board on an adjacent wall that had the monthly metrics in diagrammatic form.

I waited until they had finished then approached Brian. He was pleased to see me, he said "Hello Ralph, what did you think of our morning meeting?"

"Morning Brian, I thought it went very well. Everyone seemed to be prepared and it was short and sweet, just like it should be".

Brian said "That's good of you to say so Ralph, but I am sure we can improve".

"That is always the case Brian but we have bigger fish to fry at the moment".

He laughed. "So what are we doing today?"

"Well, I thought I would give you and Mal a rundown of what we have got so far and draft an update for Leon so that we can keep him in the loop".

Brian replied "That sounds like a plan. Mal has just gone back to his office, so let's head down there and have a quick catch up".

So we set off to Mal's office. He was talking to a couple of the area supervisors that I had seen in the meeting so we sat down at the meeting table and waited until he had finished. I then gave him and Brian a quick update on all of the data that we had gathered so far including the spread sheet that I had started to compile from the accounts system. They were both pleased with the progress. Mal said "Now that we have all of this data, what do we do with it?"

I replied "That is the next step Mal. First we collect the data and then we analyse it. We might find that when we start to analyse the data we come up with insights that were previously hidden that we will need to validate. There will also be things that don't make sense, so we will have to go back round the loop again. We have to fully understand the factors that affect output before we can move forward".

Brian said "What sort of things are we looking for Ralph?"

I scratched my chin and said "I think we should ask them why we get good days and bad days. What happens to create each of those situations? I think we should ask them what stops us from achieving the output targets and what would they change right now to make it improve on a consistent basis".

Mal said "OK, shall we do the rounds again?"

"Yes, but who should we be talking to this time around?"

Brian said "I think we should ask the area supervisors and team leaders in each area. They will be the ones that are closest to it all. But we must make sure that there is no blame attached to any of this otherwise they will clam up. We must make it clear that we are looking at the issues and not the people".

I looked at Brian thoughtfully. He was impressing me more each day. I said "That is spot on Brian. None of this has any blame attached – we're simply trying to understand what is going on so that we can figure out how to get a better result".

Brian smiled and said "So I think your questions should also include a bit of a script to tell each person what we are doing and how we are going about it. That way we will be able to get on with it pretty quickly".

"Agreed. I will go and write up the notes and script now and perhaps you and Mal could draw up the list of people to speak to while I am gone. I'll be half an hour if that's okay?"

Brian said "That will be fine. Come back here when you are ready and we will sort it out".

I scampered back to my office to write up the notes and make some copies. When I got back to Brian's office they were both waiting for me.

Brian said "Here is the list, Ralph. I have put the names of the people down the left followed by their location and who is speaking to them".

"Great, looks like we are all set. Shall we catch up again after lunch and see what we have got?"

They both nodded.

As I was working my way through the list, I realised that once again some themes were emerging and I was also finding out in detail what made each department tick. They all had their own ways of working, setting targets, and measuring performance. There were lots of little things that affected how they could perform, some within their control and others not. For example, there were trolleys in some departments that were used to move the vehicles around the shop floor. When there were shortages and the vehicles were parked up there would quite often be a shortage of trolleys because the system was not designed to account for the non-availability of parts. They would then start to cannibalise vehicles to get parts off one car to finish another car to free up a trolley – then it was difficult to keep track of which parts were missing and it all became a bit of a mess.

There were similar issues in all of the areas. When all of the parts were available in the right place at the right time and all of the people were available and ready to do the build then there was the possibility of some great numbers. When all of those conditions were not in place then it very quickly tailed off into something very different. The non-standard way that the vehicles were designed did not help things. For example, there were so many different wiring harnesses for these cars. Each harness accounted for the options that were on that particular car. I was beginning to think that there should only be one harness which allowed for every option and it could be the same one in every vehicle. It would be a little bit more costly, but it would make it easier to produce more vehicles.

Then there was the process itself: the 'bespoke' assembly of each car, which Leon saw as a non-negotiable because it was what he had sold to the public. I thought that there might be a way to approximate an assembly line, while still having every car hand built. There would be no loss of quality but a huge increase in output, with no WIP in the process because there was simply no room for it.

I was into resolution mode already, which is hard to stop yourself from doing when you are in a situation like this. For the time being I had gathered a whole bunch more data and it was time to meet with Brian and Mal once again. I dropped into Mal's office afterwards and they were both in there talking to one of the supervisors. I waited until they were finished and said "Are you guys ready to do a quick round up?"

Brian said "We have a bit of a situation to handle in the body shop right now – can we do it later?"

"Sure Brian. I will go and write up my notes and you can give me a call when you are ready".

"Thanks Ralph, appreciate it". So I went back to my office and wrote up my notes. It was a lot of stuff to condense into a summary but I did my best to get it into good shape. I started by creating a table which looked like this:

Data Gathered	Source	Time Span	Detail	Comments
Output Data per area	MB accounts system	Last 3 years	Actual output converted into FVE	May be open to interpretation
Output information and insights	Robert Cullen Master Planner	Last 3 years	His opinion on the output for each area	Good background
Target vs actuals per area	Area Planners	Last 3 years	Output data in the units of the area	Objective view by the planners
Output figures per department	Team leaders and supervisors	Last 3 years	Output data per area plus insights	Some reasoning behind the output

It seemed like I had a lot of data and information about output in overall terms, I had the data for every area, and lots of insights into the reasons why the numbers were in this condition and what affected the output. It was a mix of data and information, some of it quite subjective.

There was one thing that was bugging me – the common theme of parts not being available. I had got some insights from Robert Cullen, but I decided to go and speak to Alan Matthews to get from the horse's mouth exactly what was happening. I gave him a call to ask if he could speak to me for a few minutes and he agreed straight away, so I grabbed my notebook and went over to his office. As I arrived, Paul Howard was leaving. He nodded curtly and seemed to be in a hurry.

I went in and Alan was looking a bit frazzled. I asked him "Is this a good time Alan? I could always come back if you like".

"No, it's fine, Ralph. This is how it is most days at the moment so let's get into it".

I told Alan what I had found so far and how I had gathered the information. He agreed with everything that I had done and the data that I had gathered to get to this point.

I asked him "What's happening with this common theme – that parts are not available to complete the build?"

"Well, there is no denying that there are lots of vehicles around the place that are unfinished because the parts required for them are not here. I think we have got ourselves into a real mess and it's hard to find a way out".

I said "That's why I'm here, so can we try to work out what is happening?"

Alan said "Sure, we can, but this will take a while. How long have we got?"

"Well I've probably got an hour right now, and then I have to go and see Brian and Mal".

"Okay, let's see what we can do".

With that he got up and started to sketch out the process on his flip chart. He drew each department as a box with inputs and outputs.

He said "In the early parts of the process, things are easier to manage as the materials are fairly generic – steel, welding rods, and so on. So we don't have a lot of issues in those areas".

I agreed with that assessment, as I had seen it for myself.

"As we go through the process we get more complexity and the parts become more specific and are allocated to each vehicle by works order number".

I said "That seems to be an issue for lots of people, Alan".

He said "It is an issue for me as I have to treat each vehicle like a mini project and co-ordinate the delivery item as if it is part of a kit that can only go into one vehicle. Once that item is allocated in the Materials Requirements Planning or MRP system, I can't use it on any other vehicle. It is totally unnecessary and it's making life incredibly difficult for everyone".

"So if every vehicle was to go through the whole process with no identity, it would make life easier?" I asked.

"Well, sort of. I think it would make things a lot simpler if any item can go on to any vehicle without necessarily being allocated. There needs to be a proper rethink about how we plan, how we allocate stock, how we build the vehicles, and how we create the vehicle identity – and when in the process we do that".

I was beginning to understand his world and it did not seem like a good place to be. I asked him "Is there anything else I should know?"

He looked at me thoughtfully and said "I assume that I can talk to you in confidence?"

"Of course you can Alan, if you want to take something off the record then it will be perfectly safe with me".

"Okay then, I can tell you in confidence that it doesn't help that we can't pay our bills. Our suppliers are losing patience and confidence in what we are trying to do, and they are starting to make life difficult for us. We really need to have an injection of cash to unlock all of this or it is going to get a lot worse very quickly".

That made me sit up. I said "How long has it been like this Alan?"

He said "It has been getting steadily worse for a while now, but these last six months have been terrible. I have to juggle the balls every day just to keep the place fed with components".

"So let me try and feed back to you what I'm hearing" I said. "It sounds to me like we have a process that is too complicated and complex. It is set up in such a way that parts allocation to specific vehicles is making it worse. Once you have allocated parts it is very difficult to use those parts on any other vehicle, even if the other vehicle is in front of it in the queue and could be completed. We have a factory full of WIP which is eating cash at an alarming rate. We probably have all the parts that we need but they are tied up in cars sat in WIP that cannot be completed. If we could complete all of those cars and come up with a simpler way to manufacture then we could probably have a much smaller factory with a much simpler process and a lot less WIP. To top it all off, that would also mean that we could potentially finish maybe two or three times as many cars in a week as we are currently doing. Does that about sum it up?"

Alan looked at me in amazement. He said "For a guy that has only been here a few days you have got a remarkably good handle on things very quickly. If we can do what you have just said then this business will absolutely fly. I want to be part of this initiative, so you just call me and I will do whatever it takes to see this happen".

"Alan that is exactly what I wanted to hear. And don't worry, we'll get this thing sorted out, and you'll be on the team that gets it done".

We continued to explore the options for the next 30 minutes, and I was starting to spot some potential ways out of the maze. I checked my watch and said "I am going to have to go and see Brian and Mal. Let's pick this up again in the next few days and see where we get to".

"Okay Ralph, I am looking forward to it".

I picked up my notes and went to see Brian and Mal. I showed them the table that I had put together and the pile of notes that I had gathered, along with the giant spreadsheet. I also gave them a debrief of my conversation with Alan Matthews, and some of my own insights into how we could find our way through all of this.

Mal asked "Do we need to collect any more data Ralph? Seems like we have got more than enough to be going on with".

"I think you are right Mal. We probably need to start analysing this to see what we've got. But I need to let Leon know where we are up to before we move to the next step".

Brian said "Would it help if we come with you, to give you some moral support and let Leon see that we are working as a team?"

I smiled and said "That would be very welcome, Brian. Do you want to give Leon a call now and see if he's available?"

Brian gave Leon a call and he was free so we set off to see him. When we got to his office he was on his walking desk while taking a call. He motioned for us to sit at his meeting table, and joined us a few minutes later. "You know, sitting is the new smoking. I got the walking desk about a year ago and I feel so much better now, it gives me so much more energy. So what have you got for me?" he asked.

I started: "We have done a lot of data gathering the past few days. I have spent time with Martin Kirkbride and Alan Matthews, I've interrogated the accounting records system and created a huge spread sheet of output data by area going back three years".

I nodded at Brian who said "Mal and I have been helping also. We have been around all of the team leaders and supervisors and got their locally published data from the morning production meetings. We have also gained lots of useful insights into what affects the numbers".

Leon looked thoughtful and asked "Do you have a few words to summarise what you've found?"

I replied "We are starting to see lots of themes emerging, but there are two clear aspects that we can tell you about right now. One is that we are constantly running out of components for each vehicle in part because of the way that we plan and the way that we create an identity for each vehicle from the moment we launch the works order. This is hampering our ability to complete vehicles and it is causing WIP to be created in huge numbers. We believe that the process needs to be simpler and we need to design it in such a way that it doesn't create any WIP. If we do that then we will give the business a massive boost in cash and improve output by 2 or 3 times. It is early days and we still need to go through the creative process, but that is where we are up to at the moment".

Leon seemed satisfied with that answer, and said "Parts availability and reduction in WIP leading to improved output and release of cash. That sounds like a good track to be on. Is there anything I can do to help?"

"Not at this stage, Leon. We just wanted to let you know where we are up to. We will now start to analyse the data that we have gathered and if that throws up anything unusual we will come and talk to you".

"Okay guys, it looks like you are all working on the right stuff. Keep me in the loop and let me know how you are getting along".

We got up and headed back to Brian's office. When we got there we had a quick recap on the discussion with Leon. We were all pleased with the outcome and his endorsement that we were on the right track was important for us. Tomorrow would be the start of our analysis.

Brian said "Leon has been very supportive up to now and you have seen the best of him. He is not always like that. His standards are incredibly high and when he wants something done by a certain time you had better make sure it is done. He can be very demanding. That is why we are all here – because his own personal drive has brought the business to this point. If we promise to do something, he'll remember it and hold us to it whether things are going well or not. Just a heads up, so that there are no surprises".

I responded "Thanks for that Brian, I'll remember your advice".

That night Maricel was in a much better mood. I told her that the bank had confirmed an overdraft extension, so we could get the bills paid and take the pressure off. She was pleased with this progress and I even got a cuddle on the sofa.

I was woken up at 3am by the sound of running water. I dragged myself out of my deep sleep and wondered what was going on. The house was dark and quiet except for the sound of running water. I got up slowly and put on the bedside lamp. I walked slowly out onto the landing and the sound got louder. I opened the door to the bathroom and a torrent of water gushed out and ran all over my bare feet and down the stairs. I came to my senses and put the landing light on. There was water gushing out of the pipe behind the toilet and it looked like it had been running for hours. This was all I needed!

I ran down stairs and into the utility room. The stop tap for the water was under the counter next to the washing machine and I got down on my knees and reached in to turn it off. It was really tight, as it hadn't been moved for years; but after some grunting and heaving I managed to shut it off. As I walked back through the lounge I could see that the water had come through the light fittings and the ceiling was starting to sag. This was going to cost a fortune. As I came to the bottom of the stairs I looked up and there was Maricel at the top of the stairs, looking down at the whole mess. She rubbed her eyes and said "Just what we needed" and she started to cry. I ran up the stairs and took her in my arms. I said gently "Take it easy, honey, we'll sort this out. It's only a water leak. There is not a lot of damage and I can fix most of it myself".

She was sobbing. This was not like her and I guessed that things were getting on top of her. My marriage felt fragile and my life was in a very strange place. New career, no money, spending my last cash on a consultancy course, it all must have seemed like her world was being turned upside down. This water leak may have been the straw to break the camel's back. I tucked her up in bed and got to work fixing the leak. I was used to mechanical things and fixed it quickly. The lights and ceiling downstairs would have to wait for now. I went back to bed with Maricel and I looked at the clock. It was 4:35 already and I was getting up at 6am. I just hoped I could get an hour's sleep or I was going to be a wreck when I turned up for work in the morning.

The next day before I went to work I called my mother and asked her if she could loan me some money to pay for the repairs. She was exasperated, as she had loaned me some money already, but I promised that things were turning around for me, so she agreed. I thanked her profusely and told her I would pay her back as soon as I got my first pay packet. She was a real lifesaver, and I told myself to visit her more often. There were a lot of things that I was promising myself lately. I was beginning to think that I had let a lot of things slip in my personal life and it had all happened without me really noticing. It was like a spiritual awakening. I could see how I had allowed myself to fall into very bad habits. I was neglecting my own physical and emotional needs; and even worse, I was neglecting those that I loved the most. I suddenly realised that I would have to change my ways if I was to get the life I really wanted.

The next day saw me at my desk a bit late, as I decided to get some extra sleep so I could be more productive during the day – even a good habit like waking up early can be done in moderation! I wanted to get a good start on the analysis and the best way to do that was to start creating the graphs with the trend lines. I opened the spread sheet that I had created from the accounts system and looked at what I had. I realised that I could simplify the views so that I was only looking at relevant numbers, so I set about getting this done. I kept the original data intact and did a whole bunch of copying and pasting to create simpler views using the original data. I was showing not only the output data but also additional things like headcount and value of WIP for every vehicle which was very bad. Virtually every single vehicle was late to some degree.

By lunch time the graphs were coming together really well. I had added in the data received from Brian and Mal and also from the supervisors and team leaders. This allowed me to start to deduce some additional data such as output per employee per department which was previously not shown.

I called Brian and told him where I was up to. I asked him "Do you and Mal want to come and have a look at what I have done so far and we can decide where we go next?"

They came in together 30 minutes later and I showed them what I had done.

Mal said "This is looking good Ralph, though I think we should make it a lot more visual. Can we print out the graphs on A3 and put them up on the walls in here so that we can compare everything at a glance?"

"Sure, it will also give us the chance to spot what else we need and what's missing".

"Okay then Ralph, do you want to do that first and then we can come back and go through it?"

"I will do that, Mal. Give me an hour or so and it will be done".

I got to work printing out everything I had done so far, plus digging out a lot of the stuff that I had already had printed from last week. I filled the end wall in the meeting room with the graphs and I got a load of coloured pens so that we could mark up our comments on the prints.

When the guys arrived back at my office I was waiting for them.

We started to look at the graphs and Brian said "This all looks great Ralph but what do we do with it?"

"Good question Brian. I think we should all try to write messages on each graph to describe what is really happening. For example, the first graph is showing overall output of finished vehicles over the last 3 years. I can see that in year one the output was consistently rising. In year two it flattened off and in year 3 it actually declined slightly and continues to decline as the year goes on".

"Ah I see what you mean. Okay, let's all put our comments on each graph and see what we come up with. I am assuming that it is okay if we have different interpretations or views of what we are looking at?"

"That's what I am expecting. We will not all take the same messages away from this exercise and that is where I believe that the value lies".

We all started in different spots to give ourselves some space, and we started to write on each graph to describe what we thought the key message was for each one. We each used a different coloured pen to show who had written the comments.

After a couple of hours or so we were all finished writing and the graphs were totally covered in different coloured comments.

We all stood back to admire our handiwork and Mal said "That was a good exercise, Ralph. It really made me think about what I was looking at and what it was really telling me, probably for the first time if I am honest".

I said "That is exactly what it was supposed to do".

Brian said "So what now?"

"Well I think we should capture all of the comments and compare what we have got so far" I replied.

Brian said "If that is the case I think you are going to need some help to do the transcribing and to tease out any hidden messages. How about I get one of our interns to give you a hand?"

"That would be really great, I would appreciate the help".

"Okay leave that with me and I will get you some help for tomorrow".

With that they both headed back out and I was left alone with my thoughts. I started to look at the graphs and a typical example looked like this:

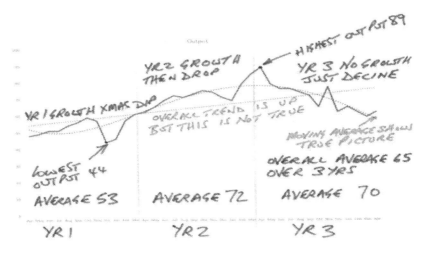

There were a number of comments on each one and they did not always agree with each other. For example the simple trend line showed a consistent move upwards which is a good thing. However if you look at the moving average it shows a very different picture. You can see that year 1 shows consistent growth with a dip at Christmas time, presumably due to the Christmas holidays, maybe there was a factory shut down? Then year 2 shows a good period of growth to reach a high point of 89 units per wee, but then it drops away quite sharply and year 3 continues with the decline almost back to year 1 levels. What happened at the end of year two to cause the decline? Also if we could previously produce 89 units in a week, then why can we not get anywhere near that number now? This was starting to get interesting and I was beginning to think that we would need to dig a bit more to get to the real truth behind the data. But that would have to wait until tomorrow.

Next morning just as I was getting engrossed in the analysis there was light a tap on my door and a stunningly beautiful young Asian girl came in. She was above average height with straight jet black hair that hung down to her waist and she had the most dazzling smile with beautiful white teeth. She smiled confidently at me and said "I am Sarah Simpson-Ling. Brian sent me to help you with some graphs". She held out her hand.

I jumped up and shook her hand, which felt surprisingly strong, and said "Hi Sarah very nice to meet you. I am Ralph Hill and I am here doing some consulting work for the business".

She said "I know who you are, Ralph. Everyone in the place knows who you are after the communication session the other week. We are all waiting to see what you can do for the business So how can I help?"

I explained to her where we had got to in the process and what we had done to gather the data so far. I said "What I would like you to do is to take all of the comments on every graph and compile them into a list. As you are doing it please look at the comments and see if there is anything else that comes to mind". I showed her the example I was just looking at and explained the questions that I had come up with as a result of seeing the comments on that graph.

She seemed to understand straight away what I wanted and said "I am a statistics graduate, so this is bread and butter for me. I will get right to it. I guess if I start to spot themes then I should group the comments into those themes to keep them consistent and in the right place?"

I nodded. I could see why Brian had chosen Sarah for this job. She was not just easy on the eye, she was extremely smart as well. What a combination.

I said "You start at this end, and I will start at the other end and we can meet in the middle".

At the end of that day we were not yet finished and it was late in the afternoon so I said "Let's call it a day for now Sarah and we can pick it up again in the morning".

She said that she would be in at 8am so she would see me then. She flashed her perfect dazzling smile at me and then she headed off. My heart skipped a beat when she smiled. She really was a stunner. I began to wonder if she was married or had a boyfriend, and I had to stop myself. I was wondering what the hell I was thinking when I already had my own beautiful girl at home. I would have to watch myself in future.

It was coming up to the month end and I had to invoice the company for my time so before I went home I decided to raise my first invoice. I didn't even have a limited company set up at this point, so I hoped that they would accept an invoice from me as a sole trader. My first month was not a complete month but nonetheless the total was very pleasing and I felt a little guilty at invoicing them for £12,500 when I had only been there a couple of weeks. When I calculated what that equated to in terms of annual salary it came to £325,000 and my previous salary in my old job had been £65,000 – good for the area, but this was in another league that I had never dreamed I would be in. I sent it to Martin Kirkbride before I went home and copied it to Simon Brown as I was not sure of the protocol to follow. My brain quickly thought about how much Millikan was struggling and that I only had a matter of weeks left to turn the business around or lots of employees would lose their jobs and their shares in the business, and all the customers would lose their deposits. I rapidly realized that £12,500 was a small investment for the bank bearing in mind how much they had on the line.

When I got home I told Maricel about my day and I also told her about the invoice for my first month and she was delighted. She said "That will go a long way to getting us back on our feet, Ralph. How long before they pay you?"

"Not sure yet, but they've promised me they will get it through their process as quickly as they can and no longer than 30 days".

"Sounds good, but don't let it sit, Ralph. We really need that money", and she was smiling which was nice to see. She seemed to be in a better mood today and we had a very pleasant evening for a change.

Next morning Sarah came in at 8am as promised and we got right back into the analysis. She was asking me a lot more questions today as though she had got used to being around me which was good. Between us we were making good progress. At lunch time she dipped out for a sandwich and I joined her in the canteen. It was a light and airy space and we sat next to the window overlooking a pond with some koi carp swimming around. It was an idyllic setting.

After lunch we got back into it, and by the middle of the afternoon we had got all of the comments into a sensible order. The comments had been grouped into themes and categories, and we had made a list of other data that we would need to gather. I gave Brian a call and told him where we had got to and he said that he would come and have a look in a few minutes.

He arrived a few minutes later and he was by himself. I sort of expected Mal to be there with him. As if reading my mind he said "Mal is on the shop floor. We have a quality issue which he is dealing with. He can catch up later".

"Okay Brian, let me show you where we have got to. Sarah has been a great help in this exercise". Sarah smiled.

I then took him through all of the comments, the themes and categories, the questions that we had generated and the additional data that we thought we would need. He was impressed with how much we had got done. He said "It is a strange feeling. I have been looking at this data every day and every week in that same 3 year period and I did not see these messages that were there the whole time".

"Don't be surprised Brian – you can become number blind when you look at things every day. Also you have probably never looked at these numbers in this format over this time period and in the level of depth and scrutiny that we have applied these last few days".

"Yes, you are probably right Ralph, but I still feel a little guilty for not spotting these issues myself".

"Take it easy Brian, that is why we are doing this now" I said.

He relaxed and said "So what do we do now?"

"I think we need to test what we have and see if it all makes sense. How about we debrief Martin Kirkbride about where we have got to in the process and get his input?"

Brian said "That sounds like a smart move Ralph. He may be able to shed some light on why things are the way they appear to be".

I gave Martin a call and he told us all to come up right away.

When we arrived Paul Howard was with him. Martin said "Come on in guys. Paul would like to sit in if that is okay?"

I looked at Martin and said "This is only preliminary stage Martin we do not have anything to formally present. In fact we are going to be asking more questions to see if the insights we have uncovered make sense".

Paul Howard said "Okay Ralph, I understand the health warning I just want to see where this is headed. No need to stand on ceremony on my behalf".

So I laid out the compilation on the meeting table and described in summary to Martin and Paul what we had found so far. I then went over the questions we had raised and the additional information we thought that we would need. Martin was thoughtful and Paul seemed genuinely impressed with what we had covered so far. He said "That is very good work guys. We do not often see the data like this and it shows things in a very different light. I can understand why you have questions and I will be very interested in staying in the loop on all of this".

I said "Paul we will be happy to keep you in the loop and if there is anything we do not understand we will come and talk to you to get your advice and input".

Paul seemed satisfied with that and said "Thanks for that. I have to scoot now, but do call me if you need me" and he left the office. Martin Kirkbride was looking pleased. He said "Guys this is good stuff. How can I help you?"

"Well how about some of these questions that we have Martin?" I replied. "For example if we look at overall output for the factory it looks like something happened 12 months ago to reduce output, and at the same time head count has gone up and WIP has gone through the roof".

Martin said "Let me look at the graphs".

We showed him what we had and how we had come up with the messages. He asked questions all the way through and it took us over an hour to brief him fully on what we had found.

He said "This could actually be a little sensitive. Let me explain. Twelve months ago was when we launched the new model, which had dozens of new options on it. Since then, the business results have gone backwards but only because we cannot make the cars quickly enough. I suspect it is something to do with the additional complexity and the changes to the supply chain. The order book is full and getting fuller but we cannot seem to get through the backlog. I have not seen the numbers laid out like this before but in my mind it confirms my suspicions that the new model has been the primary cause of this downturn".

I hadn't known about that timing until now. I said "So the new model has been a great success in one respect but a real failure in another respect because it has gummed up the factory?"

"That is what it looks like to me Ralph. I am not sure how Leon will react to this as he has invested a lot of time, money and emotional effort into this vehicle and this news will not go down well".

I was thinking on my feet here and I responded "So how can we make this look like an opportunity? How can we portray this in such a way that we focus on the upside rather than apportioning blame?"

We all looked at each other as this was not an easy question. Then Sarah said "It is clear that the future of the company lies with the new vehicle. We are not going to change that. If we focus on what we can achieve by reducing the WIP, doing late customisation, perhaps standardising the option list and the process to build the cars then we can create a scenario where the future looks a lot brighter and that is a much better story to sell".

Brian said "I fully agree with that approach. There is no way that we can point to the new model as the cause of all of this decline, although we have to be able to include it in the story. We need to focus on what we can get out of this when we get it right. That is where we need to be heading with this".

I looked at them both with admiration. I said "You guys are a lot closer to this than I am but instinctively what you are saying sounds right to me. I will be guided by your experience in this area of the business".

Martin was looking relieved, he said "Okay that sounds like a sensible approach to me. How can we go about creating the scenarios?"

Sarah said "Ralph and I will do that over the next couple of days. I am used to doing this so we should make good progress. Should we come back and let you see what we have done before we move forward?"

I was pleasantly surprised at Sarah taking the lead on this. She was impressing me more than ever.

Martin said "Yes, let's do that. When you have worked out what the potential upside is and how we could possibly get there then come back and talk to me and we will work out how to sell it to Leon".

With that, we all departed and headed back to my office. As we got there Brian said "That was quite a turn up, Ralph. I am glad that we have got a steer from Martin as it was looking a bit sticky there for a moment".

I said "Sarah is the one that pulled it out of the bag Brian".

Sarah was looking a little embarrassed, she said "I just did my bit like the rest of the team. It is all a team effort and that is how it should stay".

Brian said "True Sarah, but credit where it is due, you did a good job in there with Martin".

She rolled her eyes and said "Okay, okay, so now let's get on with it!"

We laughed and Brian said "I am going to leave you guys to it for now. I want to go and check in with Mal and see how things are going with that quality issue I mentioned earlier".

"Okay Brian we will call you when we have something to look at before we go back to see Martin" I replied.

Sarah said "So, how do you want to do this Ralph?"

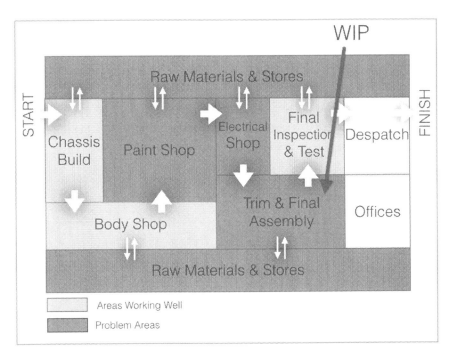

I gave her a sideways look and said "I thought you were in charge now".

She laughed and gave me a playful slap on the shoulder. I could take that all day long.

Sarah and I set about creating the scenarios from a top level. We quickly came to the view that the build process was the key. Linked to the build process was the planning and material supply areas which were critical to making it work. It also became clear that not all areas of the factory were running badly. The chassis build area seemed to be coasting and meeting demand quite easily. The body building area was a good contender, as was the final assembly area. We looked at what would happen if we removed the WIP, created buffers that worked and had parts available for every vehicle at the right moment in the build. We estimated that we could treble output with less people than were currently employed. We conceded that in order to get where we needed to be there would also be an increase in costs. For example one of the things that kept on coming up was the design and build of the wiring harnesses. There were so many variants due to the large number of options. One of our scenarios was to make the wiring harness the same for every vehicle, which would require more materials and more labour for that one area, but we calculated that it could save time in other areas and boost output overall. This was getting exciting but we had reached the end of another day. Plenty of time to get back into this tomorrow.

A Twist In The Tale

The following morning I asked Sarah to follow up on the questions that we had outstanding and also any further details that were missing while I got to work on finishing the scenarios. We were making a good team.

After lunch she came back the office with a strange look on her face. I asked her what was up, and she said "I think I may have uncovered another bit of sensitivity".

"We seem to be getting into some strange territory here – what have you found out?"

"I began digging into that time when the new model was launched. It was a difficult time because it was rushed through and not enough time or thought was given as to how it should be properly managed. It was pushed through by Paul Howard".

I opened my eyes a bit wider at that revelation.

She continued "It gets better. When it became clear that the parts were not available to meet the build at the right place at the right time, the planners requested that they reduce the load on the factory by easing back on chassis production so that we could clear the WIP and free up the cash. Paul Howard gave instructions in writing to Robert Cullen that under no circumstances should chassis production be slowed down".

I was astonished to hear this. Not only had Paul Howard made a huge mistake by rushing through the launch of the new vehicle but he had then massively compounded that error by instructing the planners not to ease back on chassis production. He had gone against the advice of a very experienced planning manager and the purchasing manager and the results were all around us now in the form of oceans of WIP. It was a glaring error of judgement, but apparently consistent with the way that he made his presence felt in the business at all levels.

This was a potential bombshell and I did not want to unleash it without solid backing from other quarters. I told Sarah that she had done some great work. I then asked her if she had tidied up all of the details and questions that were outstanding. She said that she had a couple of things to check out, but that she would be finished today. I asked her if she had found out anything that contradicted where we thought we were at this point and she said that everything was consistent with the discussion we had with Martin Kirkbride. I told her to carry on and get the loose ends cleared up and to come back to my office first thing tomorrow morning. In the meantime she was not to speak to another soul about what she had discovered. She agreed to that and set off to clear up the loose ends.

I gave Brian a call and asked him if he was free to have a quick chat. He said he would come straight up. I asked him to come on his own and not with Mal. He agreed and showed up a few minutes later.

He was in good spirits and said "So why the cloak and dagger Ralph?"

I was not smiling, I said "Sarah has uncovered some stuff that is potentially very sensitive".

He was clearly intrigued and said "Okay, tell me more".

I told him what Sarah had told me earlier and he listened intently. When I was done he said "That is politically very sensitive. You know how well Paul gets on with Leon and you know the sort of influence and power that Paul has in the business?"

I nodded. I was quite aware of both of those things. I said "Sensitive or not it is something that we will have to deal with and come out of the other side in one piece. This could explain why Paul Howard wanted to get an update when we were with Martin Kirkbride".

Brian said "You could be right, Ralph. What is Sarah doing now?"

"She is out tidying up the loose ends and getting the final details that were outstanding just for completeness. There is nothing that she has found so far that is contradicting what we discussed with Martin. I have told her not to breathe a word to anyone about this".

Brian looked relieved, he said "Sarah is a smart girl, she won't put her foot in it. Let's sleep on this and decide how to handle it tomorrow".

I was only too happy to agree. This had been a very stressful day that I was not likely to forget for a while.

I had a restless night thinking about what we had learned yesterday and I got into work early as usual, but rather more tired than I would have liked. Sarah was already there. I said "Hi Sarah ready for another day at the pleasure dome?"

"Very funny, Ralph. I was thinking about what we found out yesterday and I was tossing and turning all night".

"Funny you should mention that because I was doing exactly the same. We have a hot potato on our hands here and we will have to do some fancy juggling to keep from getting burned".

She nodded and looked thoughtful.

"Anyway, we'll have a chat with Brian this morning and decide how we should play it".

She smiled when she heard that and said "Yes, that sounds like a good idea".

So I gave Brian a call and he said to come down straight after the morning meeting.

In the meantime I went through all the loose ends and details that Sarah had tidied up yesterday to make sure there was nothing else in there waiting to bite us. It all looked good and I told Sarah that and added "I'm not sure what else you have to do just now but I would be happy for you to stay on the team until we get this thing rolling along and on track for some great results. What do you say?"

She replied "That sounds great, Ralph. I was only doing some dry accounting stuff before, so this is a very welcome break. I'm sure that if they need me back they will shout loud enough, so in the meantime I am on the team".

"Terrific, glad to have you on board" and I was genuinely pleased to have her working with me. Smart, intuitive, sensitive, raven hair, great body, beautiful…I had to give my head a shake as I started to drift into a daydream that Maricel definitely would not like!

I said "Come on. We will head down to Brian's office. He should be finishing the morning meeting by now".

So we grabbed our stuff and set off down to see Brian. He was in his office with Mal. We walked in and Brian motioned for us to sit at the meeting table while he was finishing his discussion with Mal. They both joined us at the table. Brian said "I have briefed Mal on what we found out yesterday. He is in agreement with our findings and what the data is telling us".

I looked at Mal and he was nodding. He looked serious so I knew that he was not taking this lightly.

I said "So, we are all dialled into the real situation now. How do we propose to take this forward? I like Sarah's suggestion from yesterday about focusing on the upside and not the personalities, and making this look like an opportunity rather than an attack. Is that what we are going to do?"

Brian and Mal were both nodding. Mal said "There is no way we can point the finger at anyone with this stuff no matter what we might think personally. It is too fraught with danger for all concerned. We need to make this look like we have gone over the data, identified some opportunities to improve, and come up with a load of suggestions to do that without mentioning who we think is responsible for this mess".

"That just about sums it up" I replied. "Do we need to get Martin onside before we take this to a wider audience?"

Mal said "Without a doubt. We need some heavy duty back up on this one before we go talking about it outside of this group".

I called Martin, and he told me he only had half an hour to spare right now. That was enough time for us, as we only intended to give him a quick update. We all trooped up to Martin's office. He was waiting at his meeting table for us.

I started "We found out some things yesterday which are sensitive, and we thought that you should know where we are up to with it".

"Okay Ralph, tell me what is on your mind".

I told Martin the potted version of what we had found yesterday. Martin did not ask any questions he just listened. When I was finished he said to me "And who else knows about this?"

"Only the people in this room" I replied.

"Good. I am glad you came to me first. I think that we have to be very careful about how we handle this. I am not going to put anyone in a bad light in front of Leon, especially not Paul Howard. Like it or not we cannot use this in our discussions or findings unless someone else raises it from outside of this group".

I agreed "Yes, that's what we thought also, but we wanted to get your input before we did anything else".

"So what do you propose to do next?"

I said "We are going to look at what we have found and start to generate some options to take forward. I want to debrief Leon on where we are up to, like I do at the end of every week, but I think we need to sense check whatever I'm going to say before I go to see him".

Martin said "What you have found out data wise is fine. You can discuss that with him to your hearts content. But do not mention the issues surrounding Paul Howard. Just tell him where you are up to in general and what the data is telling you about improving output and reducing WIP and so on, but leave out the sensitive bits".

"Okay Martin, I'll do that today".

The rest of us walked back to my office. When we got there Brian said "I think that you and I should go and debrief Leon together. I know him pretty well and I want to keep this low key. He is like a Zen Master – he can tell when you are keeping things from him, so it has to be done carefully".

I said "That suits me, Brian. Sarah and I will summarise our findings and then you and I can go and chat to Leon".

"Okay, let me know when you have created the summary".

"Will do".

Sarah and I set about summarising all of the analysis that we had done so far and what the key messages were. We grouped it into the themes and categories that Sarah had identified and we got it looking in good shape. We created an executive summary at the start to tell the story in one page, and when we had done all that I sent it over to Brian by email to let him read it before we went in to see Leon.

Brian came back to me after about an hour and said it all looked fine. So I gave Leon a call to see if he was available for an update. He agreed and said that we could come up straight away. We met outside Leon's office, and Brian whispered "Leave this to me". For some reason I felt like I was walking into the lion's den, but it should have been no different to any other day. It was just that this time I felt like I was not being honest.

Leon motioned us to sit at the meeting table so we sat down. Brian laid out the copies of the brief on the table and Leon came over. "So, how's my favourite rescue team getting on?" he said, rubbing his hands together.

Brian immediately took over "We are doing well, Leon. Ralph and Sarah have completed the analysis and it threw up some questions and other data that we needed to track down. That is all done now. We have run through it with Martin and he is happy that we are all on the right track, and we just wanted to bring you up to speed with that".

"Alright then, fire away".

Brian then spent the next fifteen minutes going through the executive summary and expanding on the points that we had raised. He made the point very gently about the last year showing a decline in numbers and said that it looked like the complexity of the new range had raised some issues that we needed to understand more fully. He said that the WIP needed to be removed from the factory, the process needed to be smoothed out, and the parts and planning had to be aligned to get the best possible result. No mention of anything to do with Paul Howard or any unusual instructions or bad judgement calls.

Leon was asking questions as we were going through and Brian answered most of them right off the bat without any hesitation. I played a supporting role and smiled a lot.

Leon looked satisfied and he said "This all looks fine to me. Is there anything else you want to tell me?"

My heart skipped a beat. It was like he knew that we had something to hide.

Brian said "Well it looks like there may be a double edged aspect to this Leon. We might have to add in some cost to improve output. We also might have to lose some people to get it to work better".

Leon looked quizzical and said "Can you explain that a little bit more?"

Brian said "We are not into the creative part of the process yet Leon so I may be jumping the gun a little bit, but it looks like there may be an opportunity, for example, in the harnessing area. Instead of making the 30 different variants of harness that we currently do, we could make only one harness which covers all options. We could standardise the components, and even get some of it outsourced so that it never becomes a bottleneck again. It will add to the cost of the harness but it will free up the finishing area, remove tons of WIP from the process, and improve output significantly. We will need to run the numbers but that is the sort of thing I am talking about".

Leon relaxed and said "That seems like a sensible trade off to me. But don't go and implement any of this until you have worked it through properly and you can convince me that it is the right thing to do. I'm open to this, but I'm not 100% there yet, if you see what I mean. Nothing is off limits here so do not feel like you have to tiptoe around anything but let me know what you are doing so that I don't step on any landmines when I am talking to other staff or the bank for example".

I chipped in "That sounds just fine to me, Leon. We will come back to you in a few days with our recommendations".

He smiled and we got up to leave. As we were going out of the door he said "Wonderful work guys, keep at it and we will get there pretty quickly. I can feel we are on the verge of doing something really good here".

It was good to have got that meeting out of the way. Brian had handled it expertly and we both knew that we had dodged a bullet with that one.

Back at my office we sat with Sarah and called Mal to come back up. When we were all together we started to discuss the next steps.

I said "The next part of the process is where we get creative, but that will have to wait until next week. I think we all need a break from this and to come back on Monday with clear heads. I'll do some thinking over the weekend and we will all agree the next steps on Monday".

They all agreed and that was another week at Millikan concluded. I drove home feeling like I had done some great work this week with the team but I had also given a brief to the Chief Executive and deliberately withheld information that at some point would have to come out. I could not help but think that this would come back and bite me. A part of me was thinking it would be better to stick to the facts and avoid the politics, but that was how I got fired from my old job. I had certainly learned my lesson last time, and was glad that Brian and I were collaborating on how to bring this sensitive topic through to a solution that would work for all parties.

R IS FOR REVIEW:
RALPH'S REFLECTIONS

At the end of the week I again wrote down my reflections from what I had learned and what I had experienced. It looked like this:

I had learned that data gathering and analysis is a very important part of the process, and you need team members with a range of skills to do it correctly and completely. When teasing out the messages it is good to get a number of different points of view and the data will come from many different sources and will not all be in the same format. There will need to be some interrogation of the data to fully understand what is going on and you will need to check and validate all of it before you take it as useable. Themes will emerge, and you need to gather them into useful categories.

The analysis element will throw up messages that were hidden in the data the whole time, and sometimes there will be revelations that are politically or personally sensitive. It is always best to get some senior level support for the things that the data is telling you, so that when the data is fully analysed you can then present the 'current reality' to the senior management. In many cases there will be 'inconvenient truths' that you need to either bring out or suppress depending on the situation.

Personal Life

This week I had let Maricel down not once but twice, and she had responded as expected. On top of all the stress of recent months, it now seemed like her husband had got himself a new job and completely forgotten about her. I had to get this situation back on track quickly.

I had sent in my first invoice and that felt good, but I was beginning to realise even at this stage that money was probably not going to be the biggest motivator for me. Getting my own life and my relationships in good shape was turning out to be more of a concern for me, and I could tell that my life was going to go in many new and different directions from here on in.

I had cut down my drinking dramatically by telling myself that I could have a drink, but it would have to wait until tomorrow. I had also lost a few pounds due to the number of meals I was missing and the level of activity that I was putting in while getting around that enormous factory. I was better at going to bed earlier and the green smoothie was giving me more energy in the morning and throughout the day.

All of these things were progress to me and I was determined not only to be a great consultant but also a good person and the best husband that I could be. This whole experience was turning into so much more than a consultancy course. It was turning into a life-changing and life-enhancing journey – one that I was determined to take.

To get the free in-depth video tutorial on this step of
7 Steps to Profit go to **www.90daystoprofit.co.uk/bonus**

7 STEPS TO PROFIT

3 Opportunities
2 Review
1 Problems

CHAPTER THREE

O IS FOR OPPORTUNITIES
SAM'S SESSION 3

I arrived early for the session with Sam on Saturday morning and he was already there. I told him exactly what had happened during the week and he said "That is excellent work, Ralph, and it is really good that you are expanding your team with some good people. I think when you give your brief to the group this morning, just keep it to the less sensitive areas. You might mention in passing that you are finding some interesting people dynamics but leave out the detail".

I was only too happy to agree to that as the other guys were already coming in.

We all did our brief summary and some of the guys were getting into some serious issues – it was good to see the way that the group supported each other with advice and suggestions. Sam was smiling too.

Then we got into Step 3 and it was all about generating opportunities for improvement and finding solutions. These were our potential silver bullets. This was a natural progression from everything we had done so far. We had identified the thing we were going to fix. We had gathered the data and we had been round the loop to make sure it was valid. We had analysed the data and teased out all of the messages and insights that were previously hidden and we had got sign off from the top that we were on the right track. All good so far.

Sam said that Step 3 is like the War Room. This is where the experienced heads look at the information they have gathered and start to generate a number of different ways or strategies to achieve the mission. They look at possible alternative ways to get the mission completed successfully. The commander will take on board views from his trusted aides and officers before agreeing on how to take it to the next step. The same principles applied in business – this was the creative process where potential solutions were put on the table for consideration.

The next part was to clearly articulate the desired future state of where we needed to be. In the case of Millikan it would be something like this:

"We have a process that runs smoothly and flows well. It does not generate any surplus WIP. All parts are available at the point that they are needed in the process and we never have to wait. The process is slick and standardised and is as simple as we can make it to match the customer requirements on time and in full. The company has a process of ongoing improvement to identify areas that are not matching the targets and there is a well-known and well managed suite of measures to identify this".

That is a concise statement that is easy to create but the amount of work required to get to that future state would require a lot of input and participation from many key people in the business, all working as a team to get it done.

The suggested methodology that Sam was showing us was a form of focused improvement groups that he called the Silver Bullet Generator. It involves breaking down the future state into bite sized pieces and working on it with a suitable team to generate solutions or "Silver Bullets" for each of the problems that we would need to overcome. For example if we just looked at increasing output to match the customer requirement and to eliminate the current backlog, we would need to be producing at a rate of 100 units per week for the rest of the year at least. To get to that point we had to have a build process that allowed that rate of production. The current process clearly did not achieve that rate. We had seen output figures rise steadily from the low 40's way up into the low 80's and then it had fallen back into the 70's and 60's. We were going backwards when we desperately needed to be improving.

The groups that worked on this creative process were led by a facilitator, and there was a methodology that Sam taught us to become polished at facilitation quite quickly.

Sam also taught us his take on the 80/20 rule or the Pareto Principle. He said "Pareto was an Italian economist who worked out that 80% of the wealth in the country was in the hands of 20% of the population.

He then started to notice that this same relationship existed in all facets of human endeavour, and it very quickly became a 'rule'. We use it today in our line of work to describe the 20% of things that you need to work on to make an 80% difference to the business. Unless you can identify these things, you will fail as a business transformation consultant. You make up your own mind – do you want to work on the things that will make a difference or do you want to work on things that will make no difference?" Of course we all said that we wanted to work on the things that would make a difference.

Sam continued "If you are genuine about this then you will identify the one thing that needs to be fixed and work out what levers you need to pull to fix that one thing and only that one thing. There will be lots of elements that seem to have a connection, but there are only a very small number of things that truly affect the outcome. The way to identify those things is by monitoring, measuring and observing what really happens in a business and then creating the typical Pareto graph which will tell you what the 20% is that affects 80% of the business. This means you don't waste your time spinning your wheels on things that don't matter".

When we were done I was buzzing once again and really looking forward to next week.

Opportunities

First thing on Monday I met with Brian, Mal and Sarah to let them know about the creative process. I told them that I would be running breakthrough sessions to generate what Sam was calling the 'Silver Bullets' to kill off the current problems and create a road map for a much better future for the business.

Brian said "This looks great, Ralph. How do we go about choosing the right people to be on the breakthrough teams?"

"In the short term Brian I would really appreciate it if we could have our own breakthrough session and we can decide what we do after that" I replied.

"Sounds good to me, what do you need?"

"Well I would like the four of us to review what we have done so far and decide which topic we are going to tackle first so that we can get the biggest bang for our buck. I then want to communicate that to the whole workforce, and then we can select the teams to suit the topic that we have chosen and ensure everyone is on board from the word go".

Brian said "I really like that approach. It keeps people on side at all times and we are going to be working on the issues that have the biggest potential for improvement from the start".

I replied "We aim to please" and tipped my imaginary hat. We all laughed.

"So when can we get together and do the first part?" I asked.

Mal said "We have a few pressing issues this morning so can we do it first thing after lunch? How long will it likely take?"

"Well if Sarah and I do some prep this morning we can probably get this done in a couple of hours".

Mal replied "Sounds entirely doable to me. See you at 2pm". And they left to run the morning meeting.

So Sarah and I reviewed all of the data we had so far. We looked at all of the themes and categories and we started to create some order out of what we had gathered and analysed.

We came up with a number of themes. Firstly the output of finished vehicles was too low. The OTIF or 'On Time in Full' delivery performance was poor and declining. Output per area or department was variable though, and not all departments were struggling. In fact some departments clearly had too many people and not enough work to do. Buffer stocks between stations and between departments, where they existed, were not working as they should. WIP concentrations per area or department were also variable, and WIP was not spread evenly through the process. Some areas had way more than others, which was a good indicator that that area was not keeping up with the overall process flow.

Process timing and content to meet customer requirement was clearly not balanced and there were opportunities to rebalance the process. One of the biggest issues was that parts availability to match the process steps was not in place, and this was one of the biggest causes of vehicles being unfinished. Which raised an interesting question – can we get all of these missing parts out of the vehicles that are tied up in WIP?

We also looked at the golden rules for planning and methods to allow for a continuous build process and we thought that this could be identified properly if we created a logic diagram. To go along with this concept there should be purchasing golden rules and methods to ensure full parts availability. It is a critical factor that all parts must be on site to launch every works order.

We discussed the purpose of the sub-assembly[1] build to match main build areas, and if it was sufficient to meet future requirements. It seemed like there might be an opportunity to build more sub-assemblies in advance of the main build, to make the process quicker and easier.

We thought that reducing complexity to smooth build process was an important part of the future work load. Also we could do more with late customisation of each vehicle and to create a more standard product offering. The more we could make each step the same for every vehicle the more we could standardise the build process.

---

[1] a unit assembled separately but designed to be incorporated with other units into a larger manufactured product.

There was a big job to create standard work to suit the new process. Every task must have a Standard Operating Procedure (SOP) in picture format per work station, so that training becomes a lot easier.

One of the things that Leon would not compromise was quality, so we had to ensure that all solutions that we proposed did not compromise quality in any area. We had to build quality into the process. Part of that meant that the training of any new methods had to ensure consistency at all times – who, what, why, where, how, and the resources needed all had to be nailed down for every part of the process.

If we got this right there would be a significant cash flow improvement to fund any changes that were proposed and the WIP reduction could help with this.

There had to be a way of measuring performance consistently to identify any shortfalls in any area. To achieve this we thought that we had to establish common units of measure in all parts of the process. One of the things that we had discussed was FVE, or Finished Vehicle Equivalents, which would apply to every department and was a potential way to normalise all measurements in the factory.

One of the biggest things we had identified was how to prevent WIP from growing out of control. The process must not allow excessive WIP to be built over and above what was allowed to be in the buffers between work stations. So the task was to figure out how to run as lean as possible and maintain 100% delivery performance so that output could become repeatable and predictable and accurate delivery dates could be given to every customer. More importantly the business could make a profit on every vehicle delivered.

There were lots of sub headings and categories that we believed were already covered in the high level list so we captured them separately.

We were both happy that we had covered most of the bases so we went and grabbed a bite of lunch in the canteen and we were ready for when Brian and Mal came back at 2pm.

When they saw what we had done they were both impressed. We had a good discussion about which one of these we would focus on first to get the biggest win for the business. At the end of the discussion we had decided that WIP management was what we should tackle first. We estimated there was around £160m tied up in WIP in all areas of the factory. If we could get rid of the WIP we could release that money back into the business and allow us to put more resources into the other topics. This was what the bank needed to see. WIP was the big Pareto Principle domino that would hopefully start a chain reaction that would dramatically change the course of the business and save 1400 jobs.

I was happy with this and I wanted to make sure that we had high level backing for setting off in this direction so I said "This looks fine to me guys, and I am happy that we are all in agreement that this is the direction we should be heading. I am conscious that this is also an area that is potentially sensitive so I want to make sure that Martin, Leon, and Paul are all aware of what we are doing next and to give them the opportunity to have their input before we go any further".

Brian and Mal looked at each other and nodded. Sarah was a bit fidgety and she said "I know it is the right thing for the business, so I think we need to get this approval right now and get it moving".

"OK, I will call Martin first and get his buy-in; then we can tackle Leon and Paul".

I called Martin and told him where we had got to in our discussions. He agreed that we were heading in the right direction and he was also pleased that we were going to run it past Leon and Paul before we started to create the teams. He said "In my opinion this is the right thing to do. I would get Paul and Leon together and let them know what you are going to do so that there is no misunderstanding from the start. Good work Ralph".

I told the team what Martin had just said and Brian again said that he would like to lead the discussion with Leon and Paul. I was happy with that so I gave Leon a call. His secretary picked up and said he was in the middle of a power block and would be ready for them in about 45 minutes. Two times a day, Leon would go into supersonic focus mode where he would not allow for distractions from anyone or anything. During these 90 minute power blocks he would only focus on one topic at a time. Brian said that this was part of his ability to be extremely productive. We called Paul Allen to see if he could join us in 45 minutes and he confirmed.

We got to Leon's office at the appointed time, and Leon and Paul were both there waiting for us. We had printed out our high level list and Brian took the lead. He said "Thanks for seeing us at such short notice, it is appreciated. We want to get moving on the creative process and we wanted to make sure that we have your backing before we do that".

They were both nodding even before he had finished speaking. Leon said "We are both keen to get this project moving in the right direction so what do you want to tell us?" Paul Howard did not say anything but was looking at Brian intently as if he was expecting something he was not going to like.

Brian said "Here is the high level list of topics that we have generated from the analysis phase of this process. As you can see there is a lot of stuff to get through but we are only going to tackle one issue at a time. After some serious discussion we would like to propose that WIP management is the thing to do first. We have run it past Martin and he agrees that there is £160m in cash tied up in WIP in the factory, so if we can free up this cash it will take the heat off immediately with the banks and the shareholders and give us additional resource for further work down the track".

Leon looked pleased and said "Instinctively this sounds like the right thing to do. I can see from your list that this is only the first step of many that we will have to take but freeing up the cash and decluttering the factory seems like the right place to start. We can look at creating a new process so that we do not get into this condition again once we have done that. What do you think Paul?"

Paul was quieter than usual when he was sitting next to Leon and he said "I agree. I had no idea that there was so much cash tied up in WIP, and it is cash we desperately need right now, so it is fine with me".

We were all visibly relieved to hear this. Brian said "It has been a team effort to get to this point and we are now all agreed that this is the right thing to do, so thank you for your support. We may ask either or both of you to take part in the creative process when we start putting problem solving teams together – would you both be happy to take part?"

They both agreed straight away. We were having a good day it seemed. Leon said "I am sure we will both be happy to take part if it gets the business back on the track. I don't mind investing the time or the effort into making this a positive experience for all involved. Count me in".

Paul said "I agree I would be happy to take part".

I said "Thank you both for your support. We will put the teams together and start working on this tomorrow morning. When we need your input we will give you a call to check your availability".

And with that we were on our way again. No more tiptoeing around sensitive issues; just focusing on the things that needed to be done. I remembered the words that Sam had said about Peter Drucker - "Do the first things first and the second things not at all" and it seemed to fit this situation perfectly.

Back at my office I thanked Brian once again for his handling of the situation. He said "This is a team effort Ralph and I am happy to do my part. Now let's get on with making up these teams". I grabbed a marker pen and went to the flip chart.

"Okay let's talk about how we make up these teams. We have agreed that WIP management is where we are going to start. And we already know that not all areas are equal in terms of their ability to generate and get rid of WIP. Where are we likely to make the biggest impact if we are able to remove the WIP?"

Sarah was on top of the data and she said "If we look at where the most WIP is located, it would have to be final assembly which is very close to the end of the process".

I said "That would make sense to me. It is freeing up the end of the process which gets finished vehicles out of the door much quicker, and allows more unfinished vehicles to move through the process into final assembly. It will free everything up and allow us to really move the WIP out of the whole process. Are we all in agreement?"

Mal said "It feels right to me, Ralph. If I was to choose an area without having any data that would have been my choice. The data we have collected substantiates that choice, so it sounds good to me".

Brian was nodding "I agree with Mal. That end of the whole process seems to have the greatest potential".

Sarah was also nodding "So if we are all agreed that this is where we should start, who should be in that team?"

"Well let's think about this" said Brian "What do we need to do so that the WIP is removed and we can maximise the output? I think we have to have all parts available for every car and we need to be able to allocate any car to any works order; so we need to be able to reallocate the vehicle identities as we are going along. That means we need heavy input from planning and purchasing as well as build experts from that area".

I agreed in principle and said "Brian, that all makes sense. So we need Julie the planner from that area, maybe Robert Cullen also. We need Carl from purchasing who looks after that area, and I would like you or Mal to be on the team. Sarah, if you could be on this first team I think that would be good experience for you, so that gives us 5 or 6 people so far. If we get the team leader from the end of final assembly and one of the key operators from that area also I think we will have a great team. What do you think?"

I looked around the room and they were all nodding.

Looks like we got ourselves our first improvement team:

Julie – Planning
Robert Cullen – Master Planner
Carl – Purchasing
Mal – Production
Sarah – Statistics
Ralph – Facilitator

I said to Brian "Could you arrange to have all of these people available tomorrow morning at 08:30 and we can make a start?"

"Sure I can do that. How long will we need to get this first event completed?"

I said "To be honest Brian I am not sure how long it will take. I suspect it will be at least two days, maybe even three to get it done right".

"Hmm, I'll need to ensure that we have cover for the guys on the shop floor, but leave that to me. Also I'll need to speak to Allan Matthews and Robert Cullen to get their buy-in to this process. I will come back to you if there are any issues. If not we will have our first event starting at 08:30 tomorrow".

"Thanks Brian, that is great. I am really looking forward to this".

That was enough for one day and we all headed home.

I told Maricel about my day, and she seemed genuinely pleased that I was making good progress. But the conversation quickly turned to the question of when I would be paid for my work. I was ready for this, and answered that I was sure it would not be too long. I was keen not to rub her up the wrong way tonight. This was going to be a nice, peaceful night and I was going to do my very best to make it a pleasant experience. I was learning.

Turning The Vision To Reality

Feeling refreshed and excited about the day I got up early and decided to try a new app I had downloaded for my phone called 7 Minute Workouts. I had a revelation driving home last night where I realized that just as the WIP had been building up in the factory, the fat had been building up on my belly. It was unlikely that I could fit in a one hour session in the gym every day, but I did have time to chip away at my own WIP by doing 7 minutes of exercise here and there throughout the day. Just like the problems in Millikan had compounded over time, they had compounded in my own life. Last night I had decided to use the power of compound interest in my favour instead. Here we go, I thought, as 30 seconds of pushups started.

When I got into work I was feeling full of energy from the small lifestyle changes I was implementing, with a new focus on getting quality sleep, alkaline food and water and now these mini- workout sessions.

I started the day by making sure that there were lots of sticky post-it notes and coloured marker pens for the whiteboard and the flip charts. Sarah came in and I asked her to make sure that we had all the data to hand for this final assembly area including the original graphs and any insights that we had determined since then. She hooked up her laptop to the big screen ready for the team to arrive.

Within a few minutes Brian came in and said that he had got approvals for everyone to attend, so we should be all set.

Very soon the rest of the guys started to roll in and I made them all welcome and asked them to take a seat.

Sam had given us a formula to facilitate this kind of session and this was my first time doing it in real life. I followed the formula and began to see that it was working.

First I asked them all to relax as we were going to be here for 2 or 3 days, so we needed to be relaxed yet focused. Then I set the scene by telling them that we were going to be looking at removing WIP from the final assembly area of the business, and that it was important that we have input from everyone in the group. I then told them that there are no wrong answers and no bad ideas – everything has a value in this discussion no matter how crazy it may seem. Sometimes the craziest ideas can lead to something of immense value. I told them that if they were unsure at any time, they could always ask a question and that no questions were off limits. It was important to me that they did not feel constrained or timid during the interactions.

I explained that we are here to help and we want to get a fantastic result at the end of this process. I then started to lay out what we would be doing: we start by mapping out the process to understand what is currently going on. Then we will clearly articulate the desired future state so that we can all see what we are trying to achieve. Between us we will all work out how we can get from the current state to the desired future state, and that will require some creative thinking.

Importantly I confirmed that the directors of the business were behind the initiative and would support our recommendations. This was well received.

I made it clear that if there are any enablers that we need to have in place, we will identify them in this session and identify who we need to enlist in the business to support us in getting those enablers in place.

I also made it clear that we are looking for solutions in this order: no cost, low cost, revenue spend, capital spend. That means finding the most cost effective solutions that we can.

I reassured them that this is really important work for the business and I asked for their full support and participation. And finally I stressed that in this forum we are all equal, there is no rank in this session no matter who attends.

Once this was all clear in their minds I clapped my hands and said "Are you all clear?" After lots of good-natured nodding I said "Then let's get started!" and we were off on our new adventure.

After the opening remarks everyone was buzzing and I was too. I asked Sarah to start to describe the current process so that we could understand what was happening right now. She grabbed a large roll of brown paper that she had brought in for this purpose and she asked one of the guys to help her stick it on to the long wall. This was a classic technique used originally by Japanese companies in their Kaizen events, and it would do fine for us in this kind of forum.

Once the brown paper was stuck up on the long wall Sarah took over and started asking questions about how the work arrived, how it was ordered, planned, managed within the area, and what documents or information was required to make it all work.

She asked each person to get up and write on the brown paper if they had a particular knowledge, such as the planners and the purchasing guys. We were getting along great and by lunch time the brown paper was full of notes, flow charts, diagrams and post-it notes along with examples of documents and information that was used at every process step. I am guessing that it was the first time that this had ever been done in the business and people were making comments that they had never seen it expressed like this. It was already throwing up lots of questions and giving tantalising glimpses of potential solutions and different ways of working.

We had a break for lunch and came back at 1:30 to continue the process. We started by articulating the desired future state but not accepting any limitations from the current state.

After some intense discussion, Sarah had captured most of the comments and we started to construct a vision which read like this:

We want to have a process in the final assembly area that is close to continuous flow which generates no WIP. There will be buffers in between processes as required to enable the flow. Each vehicle will not be linked to a customer until the very last moment. Late customisation will be in place so that as many processes as possible can consist of the same standard work with little or no deviations. We would like to approximate an assembly line in nature so that the vehicles move through well-defined and established build stations with the same parts available in each one for every vehicle. We want to have clearly defined times for each piece of standard work that we can measure and publish on a daily basis which will allow us to identify any areas for improvement very quickly. In the short term we need to have a plan that will enable us to reduce the WIP to as close to zero as we can manage. This will give us a starting point for the new process. There should be trigger points in the new process to manage the WIP very tightly. Golden rules need to be created so that everyone knows what to expect and what is expected of them.

It was not very elegant and it was probably a bit long-winded, but it was a good start and we decided that we could modify it as we went along if needed.

From this desired state we broke each sentence out and made it into an objective so that we could start to see what we would need to do to achieve that desired state. As part of this process we naturally listed the things that were stopping us from achieving each objective right now.

After a while it felt like we were finding all of the reasons why we could not do something, so I decided to 'break the spell'. I said "Guys, this is a fantastic list and from the outside it looks like the whole process has been designed around the works order and the works order cannot be raised unless it has a customer ID attached to it. But I see this as an opportunity to say that it does not need to be this way in the future. All of these things are not blockers – they are opportunities to do something different". It made me think of the article I had read about Leon, and how he had said that every problem is an opportunity. When he reads the newspaper, all he sees are opportunities for business ventures to solve the problems the world is having. A very different way of seeing the world.

Brian picked up the baton and said "When we say that the works order cannot be launched without a customer reference, does anyone know why and what else we could do instead of using the customer reference?"

I was delighted with this "Great questions, Brian. Just because something is done in a particular way now doesn't mean that there are no viable alternatives. We just haven't asked the right questions yet".

That got the room buzzing and one of the planners said "Ralph, I think I may be able to help with this. If we were able to leave the customisation aspects until literally the last process then the vehicles until that point are effectively all the same with the exception of the colour".

"That's right Carl, so if we were to aggregate the vehicles into colour batches and send them off through the process as vehicles that are all the same then they don't need a customer reference or specification until the final process".

"They were all getting into this now. Robert Cullen chipped in and said "So if each vehicle has an identity number that you can match with a customer reference right at the end of the process then we can achieve everything on that list without compromising what we have worked for so far".

We were all blown away by this revelation and I said "Robert, that is a stroke of genius and will topple many of the dominoes we have lined up. Does anyone know if that is possible to do?"

Carl piped up again and said "I know that the works order field for customer reference is a field that we can change. I was part of the original team that designed the user interface"

Brian said jokingly "Ah, so it is all your fault that we have got this system then, Carl?"

We all had a good laugh at this as Carl was protesting his innocence.

Brian said "All joking aside, I think that we may have a potential solution to a lot of our issues here. What it means is that we may have to do some redesign of the process and the vehicle to get what we want and we will almost certainly have to create a separate part of the process for late customisation but the prize if we get this right is absolutely enormous".

We were all tuned into this now and we wanted to make some progress. I said "I think we all agree with that Brian. So how do we take this forward?"

Carl said "I will speak to the IT wizards and see if I can run a trial using an identity number instead of a customer reference to prove the point".

Brian said "And I will look at where we can set up the late customisation area and what we would need to do that"

I replied "Sounds like we are making real progress with this. Brian and Carl can go and do what they have suggested and we will carry on with the rest of the list and see what we can identify to complement this idea".

So Brian and Carl slipped out and we carried on through the rest of the list. Robert Cullen started to blossom with this. He said "I can create a cross referencing spreadsheet for every vehicle in the final assembly area along with all customer IDs and specifications and split it by colour. I will carry out a full reconciliation of the list and determine how many vehicles we can simply reassign to a different customer ID to allow the vehicle to be released. That will free up perhaps half of the current WIP which would free up around 80 million in cash for the business. Then I will speak to the customer service reps and explain what I am trying to do. If they can contact each customer and see if they are flexible on the colour of the vehicle or the specification to get an earlier delivery, maybe that will free up another 25% which means a total of 120 million! The rest of them we will just have to do whatever we can to expedite the missing parts but by that stage we will have generated a ton of cash from selling the cars in WIP, so it should be much less of an issue".

We were all blown away again. I said "This is certainly a day for astonishing breakthroughs! Robert, that sounds like a brilliant idea. Is this something you can do by yourself?"

"I will need some details clarified by the team leaders and supervisors in the area but ostensibly it is something that I can kick off and manage through the planning team".

"Can you quantify the benefits to the business?" I replied.

"If you give me an hour I can work it out and come back to you".

"Okay Robert, go and do that and we will reconvene in an hour".

I told the rest of the team that they could have a break, and to come back in an hour. We were making real progress with this group. When there was just Sarah and I left in the room she said "That went really well so far".

I said "Much better than I had hoped to be honest".

"So want happens when we get these answers? Do we just go ahead and get these things done?"

"No, I think we should put our recommendations into a short presentation that we can give to the relevant people at the top of the business and get their blessing before we move ahead. We will get their input at every step of this process".

She looked thoughtful and said "I never thought that I would be involved in game-changing stuff like this when I was crunching through my numbers a week ago".

"Who knows Sarah, this may be a change in your career path".

She smiled and said "I think you might be right".

We spent the next hour tidying up the objectives, blockers, and enablers before the whole team came back.

They were all smiles. Brian started the report "Well I had a look at how we could reconfigure the final assembly area to do the late customisation and I think I have got a workable idea on how to do that".

Carl said "I have seen the IT guys and explained what we wanted to do, and they said that with a few modifications we can do it tomorrow".

Robert said "I have quantified the benefits to the business of getting rid of all of the WIP in final assembly and it is massive – 75% of all WIP is in final assembly, and it carries the most value as it the furthest through the process. If we get rid of all that WIP in the next 4 weeks, which I believe is doable, we will free up £120m in cash and reduce the overall WIP to only 55 vehicles in the rest of the process. We will reduce our backlog by more than half, which will be very welcome to all customers whose vehicles are late".

I could hardly believe what I was hearing.

I said "Guys this is way better than I was hoping for. This process that we are going through right now is what we call 'Generating the Silver Bullets'. These solutions that we are creating now are all potential Silver Bullets to kill off the problems that the business is facing. Let's work through all of the issues tomorrow morning so that we have a fully formed plan on how to get rid of this WIP. I want to present the plan to Leon and the directors so that they can give us the green light to implement it as soon as possible".

And with that we broke up for the day. We were all jubilant at our achievements on day one.

Brian stayed behind and said "Ralph, this has been a totally eye-opening experience for me today and I wanted to thank you and Sarah for getting us to this point".

Sarah was a little embarrassed but I just said "Brian, what you have contributed so far has been awesome. We are just doing our bit to get the right result for the business".

That was the end of day one and we had nailed it. I was pumped and looking forward to doing more of this.

For the next couple of days we carried on with the process and looked at how much WIP we could get rid of in every department. We created around 20 Silver Bullets and we were totally on fire. Half way through day three we had reached a natural break and I called them to order and said "Guys we are reaching a point now where we have to sell our ideas to the directors. I have invited them to come here this afternoon at 4pm for a 30 minute presentation. I want this team to do that: these are your results. So I want us all to agree which of these ideas we are going to sell them. We have quantified the benefits and we now need to get the green light to continue. I want you to spend the next couple of hours putting together some form of presentation for these guys at 4pm. The format is up to you. It can be PowerPoint, it can be walking them round the room and showing them the process mapping and other stuff we have done, it can be flip charts describing the process and what we have come up with. It is up to you".

Brian took charge at that point. He got the guys into a huddle and discussed what they were going to sell and how they would do it. They decided on a mixture of slides and practical demonstrations. Every team member was given a task to do and they were word perfect when the directors turned up at 4pm.

I opened the proceedings and welcomed them all. I then handed over to the team and they all got up and did their bit. I was immensely proud of what we had all achieved these past few days and I was proud of every team member as they got up and did their part in the presentation.

At the end of it all Leon said "I am just blown away by what you have identified this week and the potential solutions that you have come up with to save Millikan. This creative process surely does work, and it demonstrates to me the power of teamwork. You have my full support to continue this work and take the business to a better place. If you need any help in creating the right conditions to make this work then get me involved immediately and I will make sure that you get what you need. I know that you cannot do all of this at once so I am assuming you will prioritise which of these 'Silver Bullets' to implement first and work your way through the list as you get your results on the board?" He looked at me when he said this and I nodded. He continued "I am impressed by the application you have all shown this week and I am sure that we will see the benefits flowing through very quickly. Well done to all concerned", and with that he applauded the team and the other directors joined him in smiling.

We were feeling pretty smug when Martin Kirkbride got up to say a few words – and he was not smiling. He cleared his throat and began "I would just like to say a few words. I would like to echo what Leon has just said. I think that this has been a great example of what can happen when you tap into the power of teamwork and I am impressed with what has been achieved this week. However, there is a certain sense of urgency attached to this work that was not there before. I had a call from Simon Brown at the bank this morning. His senior managers at head office are getting more and more impatient and it´s not helping their confidence in us when our failings are consistently in the news. They need to see tangible results in the next two weeks or they will be looking at our finance facilities with a lot more scrutiny. Simon is backing us and is fending them off but the pressure is starting to mount. Whatever you guys do now, it has to be done extremely quickly. Sorry guys, but that is just how it is. You have my full support but please get me some real results, and quickly".

And with that he sat back down. I looked around the room and saw the heads starting to drop so I jumped up and said "Martin, that is a great message. It is just the sort of incentive we need to get moving. This team will not let you or the business down. How about you inform Simon about what we are doing and why it will work. That will put them at ease I believe".

That perked them back up again and the directors all got up and left. Paul Howard interestingly did not say a word.

When I got home that night, Maricel was very sombre. We had dinner quietly and sat down together to watch a movie. When we were both comfortable, she said "Ralph, I have some news" and she looked very thoughtful. She continued "I saw Doctor Patel today and she told me that I am 8 weeks pregnant".

I jumped up and said "That is fantastic news! I'm delighted!"

Maricel did not move. She said "I hope that I am bringing this baby into a stable family environment that gives them the best start in life. I was not sure how to discuss this, but I have been so touchy just lately and now I think I know why. My hormones have been all over the place".

I jumped on to the sofa next to her and took her in my arms. I said "Honey, this is the best news I have ever had and don't you worry about anything. This will be fantastic for all of us – I'll make sure of it".

O IS FOR OPPORTUNITIES: RALPH'S REFLECTIONS

What a week this had been. So many things crammed into 7 days. Here are my musings:

This step it involves setting up a problem solving group. You have to choose the team members carefully based on what they can bring to the process and then you can state the terms of reference. The start of the creative process is to articulate the current state and then to spell out the future desired state. Next you should break the future state into bite sized pieces and decide which one to focus one so that you can start to apply the creative process. First you would identify the blockers and enablers and look for ways to unlock the puzzle and solve as many issues as possible in one move. This is not always achievable, but it is surprising how many times you can come up with a solution that solves many different issues all at once.

It is important to use the creative skills and experience of the team members so that you can make progress quickly and effectively. During this phase you will identify the 'Silver Bullets' which are the creative gems you will use and then you must decide which one or ones to use going forward.

At this stage you should think about selling the concept to the senior team and to do this you will need to enlist help and use the expertise wherever it may be, especially the team members and those that have been part of the process so far.

Personal Life

This had been a rollercoaster of a week in my personal life. It had been a quiet week with Maricel and I thought that things were still a little tense between us, until at the end of the week she had given me some news that was truly joyous. I was going to be a father. In some respects I was totally delighted with this news. On the other hand I was starting out in a new career and I had no idea how long my current contract would last or how long it would be before I got my next assignment. I could find myself looking for work again in a few weeks' time. Despite my brave face to Maricel, inside I was really stressed out when I thought about the details. Our finances were still very shaky. I still owed Sam £5000 which I didn't have yet, I owed my mother money for repairing the damage from the water leak, our bills had continued to come in and our overdraft had continued to grow. Apart from that everything was just fine and dandy. "Best not to think too much" I told myself, and this time I think I should take my own advice. I realized that just like Leon turns every problem into an opportunity I was going to focus all my attention on what I could do to make things happen. I had figured out nutrition, exercise, and the importance of sleep. I started the next page of my journal with: "What can I do to secure future work…"

To get the free in-depth video tutorial on this step of
7 Steps to Profit go to **www.90daystoprofit.co.uk/bonus**

7 STEPS TO PROFIT

4 Fine Tune

3 Opportunities

2 Review

1 Problems

C H A P T E R   F O U R

F IS FOR FINE TUNE

SAM'S SESSION 4

I was pleased to get into the session with Sam on Saturday. This was going to be a good time for me to get some practical advice on what I should do next. But he was not there early like normal, so I had to wait. He turned up only a couple of minutes before the session was due to start, so I had no time with him before we kicked off. That got me off on the wrong foot for this session. Sam said "Okay guys, it must be getting really interesting for most of you by now. Let me hear your updates and then we will get into the meat of this session".

So we all gave him a quick rundown on where we had got to. He left me until last and then said "Ralph, how did you get on last week?" This was my chance to get some input from Sam so I took a little longer than normal to give my update. I told him that we had made great progress with lots of potential silver bullets, but that we had now been given only two weeks to get things moving in the right direction or the bank was going to take serious action. Sam listened intently and then said "That is a fairly typical situation Ralph. When you are in the pressure cooker, this is what you have to expect – and you still need to be able to get a great result. Stay behind at the end and we can have a chat about it".

That made me feel a lot better. Sam said "So what is step 4 guys?" and we were off into the session. We learned that Step 4 is all about selecting one or more of the options that we had generated in step 3. In my case, we had almost selected an option by default which was to get rid of the WIP in the process. We were forced down that road by the pressures of the business, and while it felt like the right thing to do, it did not feel like we had gone through the right process to get to that point. I decided to speak to Sam about it separately.

Sam explained to us that there were many factors when deciding which option to choose, but the overriding issue in his experience was to select an option that had the full support of the both the team working on the issues and the senior management of the business. This could be achieved through sensible discussion, and in some ways it did not matter if it was the 'best' solution or the most elegant. All that mattered was achieving consensus on the one thing that the business should do at that point. In our case this was definitely true as we had managed to find a solution, albeit a temporary one, to the WIP problem that had the full support of everyone involved. We all knew that we had to get rid of this additional stock and free the cash that was tied up. And we all agreed that we had to do this before we could move on.

He said that it was very common in a mission to have several options in front of you. The 'team' could be other officers, NCOs, sergeants, and other specialists, and they would all discuss the relative merits of the various options until it became clear that there was a preferred way forward. It was very similar to the business situation in that action would not be taken until the team were all agreed on the solution that would be the most appropriate for this particular mission. In these situations there were usually lives at risk, so decisions were never taken lightly. If there were any strong objections at this stage they would not move forward until they had been thrashed out to the satisfaction of everyone in the team. I could see that it was exactly the same process as we had just gone through at Millikan.

At the end of this session I was feeling a lot better. We had covered most of the issues that I was facing at Millikan. But there was something nagging at me about the order of things to come and I was pleased that I was going to have the chance to speak to Sam personally. The other guys made their way out and I sat while Sam was tidying up, then he came over and said "You are making fantastic progress at Millikan Ralph, but I can understand why you are feeling the way you are right now. You are wondering if you can handle this pressure and this amount of responsibility on your first assignment. Am I right?"

"You are dead right, Sam. It is great when things are going well and you have plenty of time to implement changes in a sensible fashion. But when the pressure comes on like it is now you start to react differently and you want to start firing from the hip instead of taking things methodically. It is very stressful".

Sam was half smiling and he said "Welcome to the real world of business transformation. People look at me and see wealth and good fortune. What they don't see is the times like this – when you feel like the weight of the world is on your shoulders. I know it doesn't feel like it now but, this will make you a better person and it will make you stronger and more confident in your own ability than anything I can teach you. This is life at the sharp end, and it is making you think and act differently. It's a good thing. You have to care and not care at the same time. There was a test done on the F1 drivers and it turned out that the top 10 drivers had a much lower heart rate and seemed to be in less stress than the drivers at the lower end of the league. So care, but don´t take this to seriously either. You have a long career ahead of you and there will be mistakes made. So what! That´s how we learn".

Sam paused and said: "When I was in the SAS we were taught how to slow down our mind and get it laser focused through meditation. In the course I call it Thinking Time, but what you are really doing is meditation. I have been doing Transcendental Meditation for 20 years and I largely credit my success to the practice because it keeps me calm and focused when the going gets tough. It´s a bit like seeing the world in slow motion and you are able to do things you previously were not able to do. It´s like you get ninja qualities! I can recommend an app called Headspace, to get you started".

I looked at him with a newfound sense of realisation. It had not all been plain sailing for him either and he knew exactly what I was going through because he had been in my shoes. That was reassuring.

Sam continued: "I'm not sure you know this, but Leon and I both practice Yoga regularly. About 80% of highly successful entrepreneurs in Silicon Valley have one form of meditation practice and a lot of them do yoga a few times a week. Copy successful people and you get similar results and benefits".

I said "Thanks for that Sam, it's appreciated. I will look into both of these and if you do it to handle stress I'm sure it will work for me also. As you have said, success leaves clues. What would you do in my current situation?"

He said thoughtfully "You have successfully completed all steps so far and you have the support of the senior management team about where you have got to. What you have to do now is to decide which Silver Bullet to apply and where to apply it right?"

I was nodding and I said "That is exactly right Sam but I also feel like there is a bit of a deviation that I need to explain. We have all agreed that output is what we need to tackle and in order to do that we need to create a process that does not allow WIP to be created and which lifts the output by double or even more. But the pressure from the bank now means that we may not get the time to create the new process. It seems like what we have to do now is focus on getting rid of the WIP from the current process to free up the working capital to buy ourselves some time to do the job right".

Sam was nodding and he said "Ralph, things often work out this way. You are on the right track and the WIP issue is a necessary side step that you need to take in order to get to the right end point. What it means is that you must communicate to the whole business that you are taking this step to facilitate the release of the working capital and after that you will be back on track".

The penny finally dropped. I said "So this is not an unusual situation at all?"

Sam smiled and said "I get it all the time. You have to do what you have to do. Simple as that. But never lose sight of what you are there to do from an overall perspective. Think about it, Ralph – if you get rid of the WIP, what is going to stop it from coming back unless you create a new process?"

I thought about that for a moment and said "Nothing at all. It will start to pile up again as soon as we get rid of it unless we create the new process quickly".

"Exactly so communicate what you are going to do and then do it. Then get back on track immediately to get the real job done".

I was breathing a lot easier now and it showed. Sam said "The fact that you are thinking and feeling about it the way you are says to me that you are taking this very seriously and you are learning very quickly. I have every confidence that you will get the right result for Millikan. Now go and do it!"

I smiled and got up. Sam was a remarkable guy in lots of ways and I was very lucky to have him in my corner.

After that timely discussion with Sam I managed to give my head a shake and Maricel and I had a really good weekend despite my preoccupation with work. We started to create a nursery in the spare room and we talked a lot about how our lives would change with the new baby. In one respect it was a really positive thing that was happening in our lives and in another respect it was adding a level of stress on top of what I was already feeling and was playing tricks with my mind in ways that I had never expected. But I took Sam´s advice and cared, but not too much.

Fine Tune

Monday morning arrived and I was at work bright and early, once more feeling energized by my new morning routine. Because I was stressed out I had tried Headspace for 5 minutes in the car before going into the office and I felt as calm and focused as Sam had promised. I gave Brian a call and asked "When do you want to get together and discuss the approach and the workload for this week?"

"No time like the present, Ralph. I will come straight up".

As I was waiting for Brian to arrive Sarah came in. She was in a good mood and she lifted my mood also. She said "Morning, Ralph. I am really looking forward to getting into this project. I have a really good feeling about this" Just as she said this Brian and Mal walked in behind her. Mal said "Get in the queue Sarah we are all looking forward to this one!"

It was good to be back with the team. I enjoyed this banter, it was addictive.

I told them what I was thinking about the WIP. I said that we should focus all-out on getting rid of the WIP to free up the working capital to appease the bank and buy us the time we needed to create the new process which would allow us to increase output on a consistent basis and reduce the backlog to manageable levels at all times.

Brian was in agreement. He said "Ralph, this is exactly the right thing to do. We all know that it is not the full answer, but we have to do it now so that we get the chance to get the right result a little later".

Brian was tuned in already and I said "Spot on, Brian. We need to communicate to the whole business what we are doing and why. We cannot lose their support or our credibility so how should we do it?"

Brian said "This is something that we can do ourselves. We can create a team brief that we will give to everyone in the business. We will need to get approval from Leon and after that we can crack on and get it done. We can draft out a message that we will personally give to all team leaders, supervisors and managers. They will get a copy of the brief from us and they will pass it down personally to their teams. We can get this done in 24 hours and in the meantime we can be getting on with the removal of the WIP".

Sarah chipped in "So is this something that we can draft now?"

"Sure is" said Brian "Grab a pen and we can do it straight away".

So Sarah grabbed a marker pen and went to the flip chart. We shouted out suggestions and she started to draft the communication. After a few minutes we had this message:

Further to our previous communication, this is a message to inform all staff of our progress and current direction. The overall objective is to create a new process that will allow us to improve output substantially and at the same time prevent the creation of WIP. As a supplementary step we have agreed that we will first remove the majority of the WIP from the process by creative means so that we can release working capital from the business to improve our financial position in the short term. This is not the end game of the improvement initiative. Once the WIP situation is improved we will immediately work on creating the new process as originally communicated. Once again we ask for your support in this endeavour. Many thanks. Brian Conroy, Ralph Hill.

I was pleased with this and the others were in agreement. I said to Brian "This looks like a good draft to me. Do you want to run it past Leon?"

Brian replied "I will send a message to him straight after the morning meeting and we can get moving on it as soon as he gives us the nod".

"Sounds good, Brian, just let us know when we are good to go".

And with that Brian and Mal left to attend the morning meeting.

Sarah and I were left and I said "This seems like a good approach for what we have to do in the short term. If I remember rightly, Robert Cullen had some great ideas on how to remove the WIP. Do you want to go and ask him to start putting some meat on the bones of those ideas while we are waiting for Leon to give us the approval?"

"Sure thing, I will get right on it" she smiled and she jumped up to go and see Robert.

When she was gone I revisited the numbers on the concentrations of WIP in the factory and the final assembly area was clearly the front runner followed by the framing area. The further back through the process I looked, the less WIP there was in evidence. I decided to do a sense check on this and put on my safety gear to go and walk the process from end to end. I took my notebook and my iPhone so that I could take photographs as required. I already had permission to do that from Brian when I first arrived.

I started my walk in the chassis build area. This was a typical fabrication shop with lots of welding and grinding going on. I had to shield my eyes from the flash as I was going round. I caught up with Russell, the team leader in the area, and asked him why there was not a lot of WIP in this part of the process and he said "This is in some ways a separate process to the rest of the factory. We are building exactly the same thing every time and it is easy for us to gauge our workload. We have enough staff to keep pace with the rest of the factory without over producing and giving them a headache".

That was a really good insight for me. I said "So if the output in the rest of the factory goes up you can still keep pace?"

"We would just bring in more welders to cope with the additional demand. We have lots of empty fabrication booths here and we are only working on a single shift so we can flex up and down very easily".

I was learning a lot this morning. There was something in what Russell had just told me that was the key to making this whole thing work and I needed to figure it out. I thanked Russell for his time and carried on through the process.

In the body shop, the chassis was connected to the other body parts so that it started to look a bit more like a car by the time it came out of the other end. In this area, there was a fair bit of WIP in terms of the sub-assemblies that were used to make up the body of the car. The output of the sub-assemblies and the finished bodies was out of sync and it showed itself in the form of WIP. I understand that in this area there is the need for buffer stock to even out the flow but I was unsure as to how it all linked together.

Again I grabbed the team leader, Stuart, and he talked me through the process. The chassis came in from the fabrication shop and that formed the basis of the vehicle from that point forward. The chassis were loaded on to a central conveyor which ran the length of the body shop and as it moved very slowly through the process the floor, front end, rear end, side frames, roof, doors, hood and trunk lid were all added as it progressed through the shop. Each major station was stocked with sub-assemblies in giant magazines that were fed on to the line at the right moment to match the progress of the chassis as it moved through. So there was an amount of WIP in the magazines and there was also an amount of WIP in each of the sub assembly build areas. Around the sides of the body shop there were separate areas for building the floors, the front ends, doors etc. The sub-assembly build was out of sync with the magazines and there were piles of sub-assemblies on rolling trolleys all over the place.

I asked Stuart why this was the case. He told me "Each build area has its own targets and its own way of working. There is no connection between the build area and the main chassis line so it can often get out of kilter. The trouble is if there is a breakdown in any part of the process you can run out of sub-assemblies very quickly so we have tended to have more WIP around us to cater for that. We do not have a proper buffer management system in place so each supervisor sort of does it by his own experience. It works for the most part but we do have a fair bit of WIP and we could do with a proper process for handling it".

This was turning out to be a very good day for my learning process. I thanked Stuart and took some photos of the different areas so that I would not forget what I had seen.

From the body shop I moved across to the paint shop. I got hold of the team leader, Tom, and he walked me through his process. There was a car park full of vehicles in the buffer area waiting to go into the paint shop. I was not expecting this and I asked Tom why this was the case. He said "We need to queue up these vehicles because we run the paint shop in colour batches to minimise clean downs in between colours".

I thought about this for a moment and asked "So how long does it take to clean down?"

"It can take 1-2 hours to get everything fully cleaned. We try to run the colours from light to dark so that we minimise the time taken but it is not always achievable depending on the customer demand. We also try to aggregate as much as we can so we do all the white cars, then yellow, green, silver, blue and finally black so we maximise each colour run and allow us to be as efficient as we can. If we progress through the colours from light to dark the changeover is short. When we have to go back from dark to light that is when the big changeover takes place".

I was not expecting this. I asked Tom if I could see how they did it from start to finish. He walked me through the whole process and I have to admit that I had no idea that painting could be so complicated. The bodies were first washed and pre-treated to remove all hand prints and give the body a uniform condition. Then it was dried in a long oven. Then it was fixed to a device that they called a slave which was attached to a chain conveyor which moved through a giant tank of liquid zinc.

Each car was fully immersed and then upended so that every nook and cranny was covered in the zinc coating. Then it was upended once more so that all of the liquid could fully drain from the vehicle. Then it was passed through another long oven to bake the zinc into place. After the zinc dipping and baking each vehicle was inspected and given a very fine sanding to take out any high or low spots. Then it was blow cleaned to remove any fine debris. After that it was taken through a robot spray booth which applied the base coat and this was the first part of the process that involved some change as the base coat varied with the top coat colour. The darker the top coat the darker the base coat so this was the first part of the variability puzzle. After the base coat, it was dried in another long oven before going through another detailed inspection and sanding to get an ultra-fine finish. It then moved on through the next robotic paint process which applied the top coat.

This was the second part of the variability puzzle. It was then dried once again, inspected once again and then passed through the final robotic paint system which was clear coat. This was all the same, as every car received 4 coats of clear lacquer to give it a deep lustrous shine. The car was dried in between coats and the final finish was inspected for the tiniest of flaws. As each of the booths was free from any airborne debris the final finish was usually perfect but there was still a fall out rate at this point. Some minute speck of dust managed to get into the process and there was a rework loop where highly skilled paint techs could repair the surface to make it perfect. Of course, this added to the WIP in the process.

I could not help but think that there was a bit of a mismatch in the technology across the business. Here we had a state of the art robotic paint shop which was the height of technological achievement, and yet we had the final assembly shop which was barely automated so that Leon could give the customers that 'handmade' promise. It did not quite seem to add up.

I looked at my watch and saw that it was almost 11:00 so I headed back to my office. When I got there Brian, Mal and Sarah were all sat at my table talking. Brian said "Perfect timing. I just got the nod from Leon about the note. The only change he wants to make is that his name goes on it instead of ours".

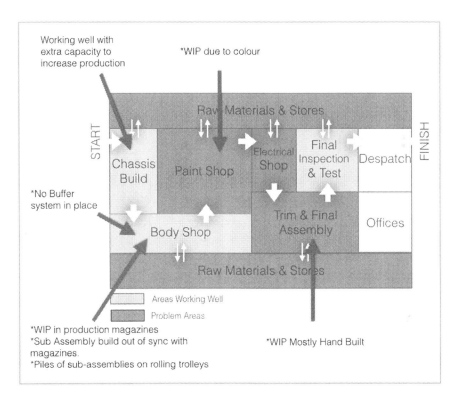

Working well with extra capacity to increase production

*WIP due to colour

Raw Materials & Stores

START

FINISH

Chassis Build

Paint Shop

Electrical Shop

Final Inspection & Test

Despatch

*No Buffer system in place

Body Shop

Trim & Final Assembly

Offices

Raw Materials & Stores

Areas Working Well

Problem Areas

*WIP in production magazines
*Sub Assembly build out of sync with magazines.
*Piles of sub-assemblies on rolling trolleys

*WIP Mostly Hand Built

"Fine for me. So how do we go about this?"

"We will gather all of the area managers together at lunch time and we can give them all the same message. They will then brief their teams and it will rotate around the shifts. We have a well-established process to do this. We just need to kick it off".

"Where will we do it?" I replied.

"We'll do it in your room, Ralph. This is one of the biggest meeting rooms we have in the business so we may as well make good use of it. I will send out a note to them all to turn up here immediately after lunch for a briefing which is signed by Leon. They will all turn up".

I was pleased with that, and said "Sounds like you have got it covered Brian. Is there anything that Sarah or I need to do?"

"Just be present when we give the brief so that you can see what happens" said Brian.

"I think we can manage that" I replied.

Brian and Mal got up and Mal said "See you after lunch and we can get moving on this".

After they had left I asked Sarah "How did you get on with Robert Cullen?"

She smiled "We had a great chat. He has just about got it worked out what we need to do. He wants to discuss it with us straight after the briefing this afternoon".

"That sounds great. How about some lunch and then we can get ready for the briefing?"

So we headed off to the canteen and had a spot of lunch before coming back to the meeting room. While we were waiting for the guys to arrive I told Sarah about my walk through the process and the discussions with the team leaders. It was as illuminating to her as it had been to me. She said "Seems like there are a number of opportunities presenting themselves already. Have you thought about what we should do when we get the WIP reduction program going?"

"I am going to spend some time with Brian and Mal and work out the art of the possible. You can help me with that".

"Okay that sounds good to me".

And with that the guys started to file into the meeting room. Brian and Mal arrived, and Brian had a bunch of papers in his hand. He called the room to order and stood in the front of the guys. He said "I just want to do a quick roll call to make sure we have got everyone".

After the roll call was done, Brian said "I have been asked by Leon to give you all this message to ensure that there is no misunderstanding. I will read out the message and I will take any questions at the end. I will expect you all to take one of these copies on the table to give your teams exactly the same brief before they leave today. You will also pass on the same message to the oncoming shift leaders. Okay?" Everyone was nodding.

He read out the exact wording of the brief that we had prepared this morning with the only change being that the author was now stated as Leon. It literally only took one minute to read the brief and Brian said "Okay that is the brief, any questions?"

One lanky guy at the front said "What is our involvement in getting rid of the WIP?"

Brian said "Great question, Dave. We are working on the specifics right now and we will come to you with exact details on what we want to achieve in each section. We will have an idea of how we want to do it, but we will get you all fully involved in your own areas so that you can give us the benefit of your experience and knowledge as we go along and enable us to get the best and quickest result. Also please bear in mind that we will be following along behind to create a new process that does not produce the WIP, so in the meantime please try to use your own skills and knowledge to keep the WIP from building up again so that we do not have to do this twice".

I thought that was a great answer from Brian. He then said "Ralph, do you have anything to add to that?"

I looked around the room and saw them all looking back at me. I said "I would just emphasise the need to get this done quickly. We have a firm deadline to get rid of the bulk of the WIP in the next 10 days so I would really appreciate any assistance you can give us which will allow us to find the quickest route through this. It is going to be an interesting few weeks so please give us your full support".

They were all nodding in agreement and Brian said "Thanks for that, Ralph. Any more questions?"

There were no more takers so Brian called the meeting to a close and started handing out the briefing notes to everyone in the room. Brian came over and said "That went really well, Ralph. I am sure that we will get their full co-operation and support on this exercise. Did you speak to Robert yet?"

Sarah piped up "I spoke to him before lunch. He will be here in a few minutes, if you want to stick around and hear what he has to say".

"Sounds good to me" said Brian.

We were just chatting about this when Robert turned up and sat down at the table. I said "Hi Robert, thanks for coming down. Can you tell us where you are up to in your thinking?"

Robert was looking quite animated which was unusual for him. He said "I have been thinking about nothing else since our session last week. I have just about worked out how to get rid of 80% of the WIP in Final Assembly in the next two weeks. It will be quite straightforward to do, but there is a massive obstacle to making it work".

He looked around and we were all on the edge of our seats. Mal said "Come on Rob spit it out!"

Robert said quite slowly and deliberately "Well, we can focus our attention on getting rid of the WIP but we may have to stop the rest of the factory from producing at the same time".

I did not realise I was holding my breath and I let it out in a sigh. I said "And how are we supposed to do that Robert?"

"That is the question I have been chewing on for the last 24 hours. I need some help on this".

I said "Okay, tell us how you have come to this conclusion so that we can all understand the issues".

Robert looked around and said "You all know that we have got a lot of part-finished vehicles in all parts of the process, but the largest number is in the final assembly area. I believe that we can get rid of the bulk of this WIP by taking people off the normal line build and doing nothing else but finishing off the part-finished cars in this area. We can redefine the vehicle identities and change the specs and do the other stuff that I mentioned last week. But if we allow the factory to keep on producing in the same way that it is now it will become impossible to manage and the WIP will build up as quickly as we are taking it away – so there will be no benefit unless we stop creating it".

I scratched my head and said "Okay I think I understand the reasoning. Do you guys have any comments on this?"

Mal piped up "I can understand the reasoning also, but I wouldn't fully agree that we need to take everyone off their day jobs to get this done. I think we can actually get a double whammy here if I am reading the situation correctly. If we bring a temporary crew into Final Assembly that have worked here before, we can get rid of the WIP at the same time as we are producing normally. That way we do not impact current output and we get rid of the WIP. We will definitely get rid of it quicker than we can create it, so we will still get a massive benefit. And if we selectively move the vehicles through the system, so that we are only working on vehicles that have all parts available, we will not create any new WIP. It means translating Robert's methodology further back into the process rather than just Final Assembly but I am pretty sure it will be worth it".

I looked at Mal with newfound admiration. I had not seen him as a thinker up to now but I had clearly underestimated him. I said "Mal, that sounds like a breakthrough to me. Robert what do you think of that suggestion?"

Robert was looking animated again. He said "I think that could work. I also did not mention earlier that there are only 6 key missing parts that are holding up a large number of vehicles. If we could engage with the suppliers in a positive way and get them to supply those missing parts really quickly we could free up even more WIP in other areas of the process".

I was all ears at this point. I said "Let me try to recap what we are saying. If we bring in a temp crew to final assembly we can get rid of most of the WIP in that area. If we change the planning rules temporarily, we can only work on cars that have all parts available so that we do not create any more WIP while we do this. And if we engage positively with our suppliers and get the missing parts delivered quickly we can also boost output and free up most of the WIP in the other parts of the process. Is that a fair summary?"

I looked around and they were all nodding. Brian said "That's about the size of it, Ralph. It is not a home run yet but it has lots of potential. In order to bring in the temp crew we will increase our labour costs in the short term and we will need to get approval to do that, so we need to work out the costs and benefits before we go to Leon and probably Martin as well. If we change the planning rules it will mean that there will be spare capacity in the other parts of the process, so we will need to understand what happens to those people and that capacity while we are doing this. The suppliers that are holding us up on the key missing parts have lost patience with us because we are not paying our bills on time and they are only releasing product to us when they get paid. We need to find a way to break through this deadlock".

"So we have some actions to make this thing work" I said positively. "If we take the positive approach all obstacles are just opportunities to get a better result".

I got up and started writing on the flip chart:

	Action	Who	When
1.	Temp crew – cost benefit analysis	Mal/Sarah	Tomorrow
2.	Change planning rules	Robert	Tomorrow
3.	Engage with suppliers	Ralph/Brian	Tomorrow

When I had finished I looked around and said "Are we all okay with these actions?"

Everyone was nodding, so I said "Then I suggest we get cracking right now and meet up tomorrow morning, straight after the morning meeting, in this room. Okay? Robert could you please send me details of the 6 missing key parts as soon as you get back to your office so that I can do my bit also?"

Robert was nodding and they all got up to leave. Brian stayed just a little longer and said "Great handling of the situation, Ralph. That could have gone south pretty quickly but you pulled it back on track immediately and made it into an opportunity".

After they had all left I called Allan Matthews and asked if he was free. He said to come up and see him in his office in 30 minutes. In the meantime I wrote up my notes from my factory tour this morning.

Twenty minutes later I got an email from Robert with the part numbers and descriptions of the missing parts. I had a quick scan and could see that these were really key parts: electric motors, dashboard mouldings, wiring harnesses, seat and interior trim sets, centre consoles and front windscreens. These were absolutely critical to the build process in a number of areas and I could see how they would gum up the works pretty quickly if they were not available. Luckily only one of the items was colour specific and that was the seat and interior trim sets. They were all leather which was good but they came in 12 different colour combinations which was a customer option to choose. I called Robert and quizzed him on the colours that would give us the best result and he said that black was the biggest selling colour by far, then white and tan. I thanked Robert for that information, which was going to be very useful in my discussion with Allan Matthews. I set off to meet Allan in his office.

When I arrived, he was just finishing with a visitor. "Come in Ralph I was expecting you" he said. He was wearing his usual careworn expression but half smiling at the same time.

I told him where we had got to with Robert and he was taking it all in very intently. When I got to the bit where I had volunteered to engage with the suppliers of the key missing parts he perked up. He said "Ralph, this is great information and I would love to help in whatever way I can. I have been personally dealing with all of these parts and these suppliers for the last 12 months as they have been so important to the business. Our relationship with these suppliers has gotten so bad that they barely speak to me now and I just have to take what I can get".

I took all of this in and said "Yes, I got that impression a little while ago in our meeting downstairs. Has anyone ever gone back to these suppliers and described what we are doing to improve the situation?"

Allan replied "To be honest Ralph, we have been so tight on cash that there was never any good news to tell them before now".

"So do you think if we laid out in detail what we are trying to do they might support us?"

"It is worth finding out Ralph. Before our cash issues these people were all on our side and trying to help but they cannot operate without cash. If we create a positive scenario for them which shows that we can help them, then we stand a good chance. How would you like to play it?"

I thought for a moment and said "You have the contacts and the relationship with all of the key people at these suppliers, so could you set up meetings with them all?"

"Do you mean all at once or individually?"

"If we do it individually it will take too long. Could you invite the key people to a presentation tomorrow?"

"Leave it with me and I'll see what I can do" and he grabbed the phone. I took that as my cue to leave and went back to my office.

Things were moving incredibly quickly and I was not even sure if I was doing the right thing. I decided to call Martin Kirkbride and get his take on things. He answered after a couple of rings and I said "Hello Martin, have you got a few minutes to chat?"

"Sure Ralph, why not come up to my office and we can do it face to face?"

I grabbed my notes and went to see Martin. When I arrived I said "I need some guidance, Martin. We have some issues with removing the WIP that we did not know about last week and we have come up with some actions. I just need to know if we are on the right track before we get too far down the road on this".

"What do you have in mind?"

I told him about our meeting and the actions that had come out of it. I said "I think we are doing the right thing but what about contacting the suppliers? I am going to have to tell them that we have an improvement plan in place and that things are going to get a lot better in the next few weeks, but I don't want to make promises on behalf of the company if I am not authorised to do that".

Martin looked thoughtful and said "I can see where you are coming from. Are you acting in the best interests of the business?"

"I believe so Martin. I wouldn't be doing it unless I thought that was the case".

"And you already have the blessing of Leon to get rid of the WIP?"

"Yes we do. He signed the note that we briefed the area managers on earlier today".

"Then you are on safe ground. What are you going to tell the suppliers?"

I thought for a moment and said "I am just going to put together a short presentation telling them what we are doing internally, particularly around removing the WIP and then creating a new process, and asking them for their support".

"So what's in it for them, Ralph?"

I was caught off guard with this one. I thought for a moment and said "Well if we get this WIP out of the system quickly it will generate a ton of revenue that we would otherwise not have. It would mean that we can pay off our arrears to the suppliers and get them on to a better footing with us going forward".

"And why should they believe you?"

"Because I can show them exactly how we are going to do it and I am happy to give them an honest update on a daily basis".

Martin looked thoughtful again and said "Do you think it would carry more weight if a director of the company were to sit in on this presentation and make a personal pledge to give this program the full weight of his support?"

I jumped up and said "Martin, that would be fantastic! Are you prepared to do that?"

"Yes, Ralph, I am. I think that this is so important to the business that I am prepared to do whatever I can to support you in this project".

"Martin, that is way more than I was expecting and it is very welcome. I will draft the presentation and send it to you shortly so that you can see what I'm proposing".

"Thanks Ralph. Do you know when these suppliers are coming in?"

"Allan is talking to them now. As soon as he has confirmed, I will let you know".

"I'll clear some space in my diary tomorrow just in case".

"I'll get on with the slides and come back to you shortly".

With that I got up and headed back to my office. As I got there my phone was ringing. It was Mal, and he said "We've worked out how to get the temp crew without taking on any more people".

I was blown away yet again. I said "Okay Mal what kind of magic have you worked this time?"

"If we only work on the vehicles that have all parts available before the works order is launched we won't have work for everyone in the other parts of the process. We can use those people, and train them very quickly to do the tasks in final assembly to get the WIP cars finished and out of the system. They are already familiar with the vehicles so the training should be very quick and easy".

I was thinking fast and I said "Will this have an effect on the working practices established by the union?"

Mal said "Already thought of that, Ralph. I am going to see Tommy Sherwin right now to clear the way"

"Do you mind if I come with you Mal?"

"The more the merrier, Ralph. I will see you at Tommy's office in 5 minutes".

So I grabbed my notes again and set off for Tommy's office. As I came round the corner next to his office I saw Mal coming the other way. Mal gave a little knock on the door and a voice shouted "Come in".

Tommy was writing something by hand and he took a moment to finish what he was doing and looked up.

"Hello Mal, hello Ralph. How can I help you?"

Mal took the lead right away and said "Tommy, we have a tricky situation and we would really like your advice to find the best way through it". I thought this was a great opening line and I promised that

I would use this myself in future.

Tommy put down his pen and said "Okay, tell me what is on your mind".

So Mal and I between us described where we had got to in the WIP removal process and what we wanted to do in terms of taking the "spare" people from the other parts of the process.

Tommy said "Mal, under normal circumstances I would tell you to take a hike and you know that. However, I can see that you have thought this through and I can also see how important this is to the business, so I am going to help you. Let me have the numbers of people, the skills and the departments of all the people that you want to redeploy. I will speak to them all and let them know that I support this initiative in the short term to get us through this particular period and then we will return to normal once it's done. Is that right?"

Mal was nodding and said "Thank you Tommy, I appreciate that. We intend to redeploy about 50 people mainly from chassis build, body shop and paint shop because these are areas that have great buffers to produce more units, but they are not needed right now. Once we have the WIP out of the way and we have generated some additional cash, we will get back to creating the new process. This is very much a temporary measure".

"I will speak to the guys in those areas this afternoon and tonight and let them know that you will be coming to them tomorrow with requests for redeployment. I assume that it will be voluntary?"

"We will tell them how many people we need from each area and ask them to volunteer. We will tell them exactly why we are doing it and what it means to the business. Effectively they will not have any work in their original area so I am hoping that they will see that it makes sense. Hopefully we will get the right number of names in the boxes. If not, I'll come back and ask for your help".

"Okay Mal, that sounds fair enough. Leave it with me".

We both thanked Tommy for his time and input and then we left.

I took a short lunch break, and as I was getting back to my office the phone was ringing again. I answered it and it was Mal again, but he sounded much more panicked than before lunch. He shouted "Ralph, it is all kicking off. The guys in chassis build are walking out. They are talking about going on strike! I need you down here right now!" I set off running.

I got down to Mal's office and it was empty. I dashed out into the factory and headed for chassis build. As I was making my way I spotted Brian, Mal, and Tommy heading to one of the side doors. I quickly caught up with them and asked what was going on. Tommy was red faced and looking flustered, he said "I started to go through the departments as we agreed. When I got into chassis build there was a bad reaction to my support for your proposal. One of the welders, a big Irish guy called Davey Maguire, took it really badly and called on his team mates to go on a wildcat strike in protest to what he called unfair treatment of the skilled people in the factory. His team mates all supported him in the heat of the moment and started to leave. As they were walking out they started gathering support from other areas and now half the factory is outside in the main carpark".

I was shocked at what I had just heard. I looked at Brian and said "What can we do now?"

Brian had a very determined look on his face and he said "Have you ever been in a situation like this before, Ralph?"

"No, I have never encountered anything like this".

"Okay, I will handle this and I will ask for you to give your input at the right moment. This is the time that you have to earn your spurs. Come with me".

We walked out of the side door and into the main car parking area. It was full of factory workers all looking hostile and I must admit I felt quite intimidated and vulnerable. This was not something that I was expecting when I came into work this morning. Thankfully it was a bright, sunny afternoon – small mercies, at least.

Over to one side was a large packing crate about 4 feet high. Brian clambered on top of it. Tommy and I followed him and stood next to the crate. Brian then took control of proceedings. He shouted "Okay guys, let me have your attention please".

The big Irish welder moved to the front of the group and shouted back "What have you got to say, Brian. And it had better be good".

Brian was totally unfazed. He said "Okay Davey, I can tell that you are all a little warm under the collar. Just take a breath and hear me out".

There was a lot of murmuring but I could tell that the guys were willing to at least listen to what Brian had to say. He resumed "Tommy Sherwin has agreed to support us in our efforts to get the business back on his feet and I thank him for that. You have all seen the recent headlines and this is the plan that will save all of our jobs". There was some jeering from the crowd and big Davey shouted "Yeah right! You guys in the office never tell us the truth! Tommy you are meant to be on our side!"

Brian again was unfazed. He said "Okay Davey, take it down a notch".

Davey looked defiant but did not respond.

Brian continued "You have all been kept up to date with our improvement program which is being led by Ralph Hill" and he pointed down to me. Again there was some murmuring but no comments, at least not out loud.

"Ralph is an engineer with a lot of experience and he has been trained by one of the best business transformation consultants in the country. He is here at the request of the bank to save the business, so please keep that at the front of your minds. I want to ask Ralph to get up here and explain what we are trying to do so that you guys can understand fully why we are asking you to help us out in this way". Brian reached down and gave me a hand up on to the crate. I looked around. Every single face in the crowd was looking at me. I was trembling inside, but I couldn't show that.

I cleared my throat and began talking. I had to project my voice to be heard by everyone which was an unusual thing for me to do. I was learning how to do lots of things for the first time just lately.

"Thank you Brian. Guys, I can understand why you might be feeling a little confused right now so let me try to explain where we are up to. Over the last couple of weeks we have made a full analysis of the business and it is clear that we need to improve output. That is not related to your performance, but to how the factory is set up to function. You have all been briefed on that, so there is no surprises. In order to improve output we are going to create a new and improved process that will allow us to produce more, while not creating any surplus WIP that eats up all of the company cash like at present. But we need to get rid of the existing WIP in the process before we can move forward. If we do this, it will free up cash for the business, clear the order backlog for the customers who have been waiting a very long time for their cars, and allow us to pay our suppliers who have also been waiting a very long time".

I added "If we don't do this, you will not have a job in 3 weeks and your shares will be worth next to nothing. Don´t do this for yourself or for me, but take a good look at the guy next to you and do it for him or her". There was some quiet murmuring going on as people were discussing what I had just said with their immediate neighbours. It didn't sound angry, so I pressed on.

"We need a temporary crew to focus on getting rid of the WIP. If we bring in external staff, it is an extra cost to the business when we are trying to reduce costs. It will also take time to bring these people up to speed, even if they have worked here before. However, because we are only going to be working on cars that have all parts available, all of the current staff in the upstream departments such as chassis build, body shop and paint shop will not be fully utilised. We thought it would be best in the short term to ask for your support in getting the WIP cleared. We would much rather use our own experienced people than bring in an external temporary crew".

I was looking around and trying to gauge the mood of the crowd, but it was not easy. Brian gave me a nod of encouragement so I pressed ahead "When I first arrived here I promised Tommy that I would keep him up to speed with what we are doing and I have kept that promise. I asked for his help today after explaining where we are up to with our improvement initiative and he kindly agreed to support us, because he could see that it was the right thing for the business. I thank him for that". With these words there was more murmuring from the crowd, but nothing too severe. I looked at Tommy and he was saying thank you with his expression. I carried on "So now I am asking you the same thing. Will you support us in getting this thing done?"

Big Davey shouted up at me "That all sounds well and good, Ralph, but how long are we expected to be away from the jobs that we're trained to do? How long are we going to be building these cars in WIP before we can get back to normal?"

I was pleased I had got this question and I responded "Davey, you will only be expected to work on these cars for 2-4 weeks depending on the progress we make. After that you can return to your original work areas. We will then work with the key people in each department and come up with creative ways to get better output without generating WIP, and we will ask you for your support while we are doing this. The main priority is to get rid of this WIP and get the company back on a secure financial footing".

This caused a lot more murmuring and another guy in the crowd shouted out "So what is really happening with the finances of the business? Do we have a secure future?"

I was not prepared for that question and I shot a glance at Brian. He leaned in and said "Ralph, I will take responsibility for this. I think we should tell them the truth. They need to be treated like adults who can handle the truth".

I said under my breath "Do you want me to tell them?" He nodded and I turned back to the crowd.

I answered the guy who had raised the issue, "Thanks for that question. I think it is very important that you all know how the business is standing financially. I cannot tell you the fine detail of it but I can tell you this. The company needs to produce around 100 cars per week to break even. Over the last 3 years we have averaged 65 cars per week and I have all of the numbers to prove it. That means that every week we are losing 35 cars worth of revenue, with the corresponding loss in earnings and profits that comes with it. The company has significant loans with local banks as well as lots of shareholder capital that is at risk. I am here to help you get the output way past the 100 cars per week and into profitable territory. I want to help you all to secure a future, not only for the business, but for everyone that works here and for your families as well. I want Millikan to be the best it can possibly be, and I am here to work with all of the key people in the business to get that done".

Brian leaned in again and said "Let me handle this bit".

I stepped back and Brian took over once more. He said "Guys, you have heard directly from Ralph what we are doing and why we are doing it. He has been honest and straightforward and I am happy to support him on this improvement journey because it is the right thing for all of us. We all have families. We all have sons and daughters who will be needing jobs in years to come and I want to be a part of that future. I would like to see a show of hands right now so that we can all get back to work. Who is willing to support us on this initiative? Let me see a show of hands for those in favour".

He looked around as the hands started to go up. It started with Tommy and then others followed suit, and very soon it was virtually everyone. Big Davey had stayed stone-faced, but as he saw the majority move in favour of the motion, he reluctantly raised his hand also. He shouted out "Thanks for the explanation. If we had got that kind of explanation from Tommy we would not be standing outside wasting our time" and he shot a glance at Tommy. Tommy was shrugging his shoulders when Brian started talking again "Thanks for that, Davey. Tommy was helping us out and I am sure that he meant well. He had a difficult message to convey and we know that things are a little tense on the shop floor right now. I noticed that we have a majority of hands in favour. Can I ask for anyone who is not in favour to stay behind please? I want to understand your issues and why you did not raise your hands. Now can you all go back to work please?"

And with that it was over. The strike had been averted and I had earned my spurs in the most nerve-wracking situation I had ever been in. Brian had handled the situation like the true professional he is and I had done my bit to get the guys back on side. There were eight people left at the end and Brian called them all into his office and we sat around the table. He asked them "So what is it that you guys have on your minds?"

They all looked at each other and then one of the older guys called Michael started to speak. He said "Brian we know that you are doing the right thing for the business, and I can only speak for myself here. I am a welder and I have been a welder my whole working life. I am a welder because it is the one thing that I am good at. I am not an electrician or a fitter, and I just cannot see myself climbing round the inside of brand new, very expensive cars to get them finished off. I don't have the skills or the inclination to do this, and I feel that if I am pushed into doing it then I will actually make matters worse and not better".

Brian looked around and he said "Thanks for that, Michael. Are the rest of you guys of the same opinion or is there something else?"

They were all nodding. A younger guy called Mario said "I am a painter, so it is a different skill set to Michael, but basically the same objection. I can't see myself as a final assembly operator. The skills are very different, and we are talking about cars worth up to £100,000, so they have to be done absolutely right".

Brian was also nodding as he said "I can fully appreciate where you are coming from guys. It is our intention to put up a sheet in each area with a bunch of empty boxes for people to volunteer. If you do not volunteer, you will not be pushed into anything. We are hoping that the bulk of what we need will be achieved by the volunteers from all areas. If it is not then we will reconvene and discuss what we need to do. You guys seem to have the best interests of the business and the ultimate quality of the product at heart and I cannot argue with that".

They all looked relieved. Brian continued "So if you are all happy with that, let's get back to work". They all got up and set off back to their working areas.

Brian looked at me and said "Ralph, you did an excellent job out there today. I am very impressed".

Mal said "I have to agree, Brian. That could easily have turned into something very ugly, and Ralph handled it like a pro".

I was feeling a little embarrassed at this kind of talk and I said "You guys played your part just the same as me. We are all in this together and that's how it will stay".

Brian said "Nonetheless Ralph, I am sure Leon will want a full summary on what has happened here today and I will tell it like I see it".

"Okay Brian, thank you for that" I said, and I made my exit.

I picked up my stuff from my office and set off home early for once. For a while I had been planning on surprising Maricel with a nice meal, and I was hoping that she would still be at work. Stopping by M&S I bought a big bouquet of flowers, a nice card, and ingredients for a healthy dinner for what was now the three of us. It had been a shorter day than usual and I didn't realise it but I was still shaking. Must be the adrenaline or something, I guessed. I sat in my car for a few minutes before I started driving home.

When I had made the dinner table nice and got the food ready I sat down to write the card I had bought for her, holding nothing back about my feelings for her. At eight I heard the keys in the door and I rushed over to help her with her bags. "You're home", she said, and smiled.

"Let me take those for you, young lady", I said giving her a kiss.

As I put the bags in the kitchen, I heard an excited squeal from the dining room. I ran over and found Maricel holding the card and admiring the flowers. A great feeling and rush of positive emotion filled my entire body.

"What time would you like your dinner, honey?" I smiled, and she smiled right back at me.

When we sat down, Maricel asked about what had happened at work. She was shocked at first and asked me all sorts of questions. I calmed her down and told her that it all worked out fine in the end and we had actually got a very good result. I was expecting to have a discussion with Leon about what had happened but otherwise it was under control. She seemed really concerned and fussed around me like I was some sort of hero. I was going to create more magic moments in our lives going forward, that was certain.

Onwards and Upwards

Next morning I met Paul Howard as I was walking towards my office. He put his hand on my shoulder and said "Brian told me what you did yesterday with the guys off the shop floor and I would like to thank you personally for your words and your actions. Looks like it got us back on track very quickly".

I was a bit taken aback and I said "Just doing my bit Paul. I am intent on getting a positive result for the business and I will do whatever is required to achieve that".

"Well, thanks anyway Ralph. I don't know many consultants who would have done what you did yesterday, and it makes me think that you might be the exception that proves the rule".

"Thanks Paul, I appreciate your kind words".

He then slapped me on the back and looked me right in the eye and said "So get back to work Ralph, and let's see some results ASAP!"

That was more like the Paul Howard I knew. I smiled and continued on to my office.

When I got there Sarah was waiting for me. She jumped up and began making bowing gestures and saying "We are not worthy, we are not worthy".

I laughed and said "I guess you heard about our little adventure yesterday?"

"Everyone in the whole place is talking about it. Apparently you did a great job of putting Davey Maguire back in his box".

"I just did what I had to do. Brian did most of the talking and I just helped out when he gave me the nod".

"That is not how I heard it. Anyway we got the right result, so onwards and upwards".

I sat down and said "That is the main thing. How did you get on with your cost/benefit analysis?"

Sarah picked up her notes and said "Well, if we can get everyone on the temporary team from internal sources then the benefit is huge and the cost is minimal. Almost zero. There will be some overtime payments that we had not factored in because the temporary team will be working shifts that are different from their normal patterns, but apart from that their cost is already being covered so there is very little additional. In terms of benefit, it is measured in two ways. One is financial and the benefit is in the tens of millions of dollars over the next 4 weeks. Not sure how quickly we can actually see the cash but I can check with Martin on that today. The other measure is customer satisfaction. We will reduce the order backlog dramatically and please thousands of customers. All in all it makes a lot of sense no matter which way we look at it".

"Great work Sarah" I said. "So it looks like there is no need to make a big justification for this proposal, just lay it out in front of the senior team and they should just say yes straight away?"

"That is how I am looking at it, but I will be guided by the views of the rest of the team of course".

I thought about that and said "Yes, I think we should get the team back together and agree on what our next steps should be".

So I called Brian and asked if the team could meet in my office as soon as possible. He said he would gather everyone up and they would be there shortly.

When they all arrived we got down to business. I asked Brian to summarise where we had got to.

Brian said "We seem now to have the support of the workforce". He nodded at me and continued "I think we should brief the directors on that situation so that there are no misunderstandings going forward. Ralph and I can do that later today". I nodded in agreement and he carried on "I know that Mal and Sarah have been finalising the numbers for the temporary crew and we will get an update on that shortly. Robert has been doing some work on the planning rules and how we can stop the WIP from being created. Ralph has been talking to Allan Matthews and Martin Kirkbride about meeting with the key suppliers and I think that may be happening later today also".

I got up and said "Great summary Brian. Do any of you have any questions?"

There were no takers so I asked Mal and Sarah to give us a rundown on where they had got to with the temporary crew. They did this at the flip chart and it all looked very plausible. Mal was going to take personal responsibility for putting the team together, and he would supervise the training and ensure that the quality standards were all in place. He was ready to go.

I asked Robert to give us an update on where he had got to with the planning rules and he told us that he had a couple of wrinkles to iron out with the IT guys but basically he was ready to go also. He did raise an important point which I had overlooked for a moment. He said "You do realise that this is going against the instructions that Paul Howard has given in writing to the chassis shop and the body shop? I know we are doing what's right for the business but we are bound to get a question about this from the people who have been working this way for the last 12 months or more".

Of course he was right and it was an issue that we would have to tackle before we pulled the trigger on that part of the plan. I thanked him for his insight and told him that we would address it before we went live with the new rules.

I then gave them all an update on where we had got to with the key suppliers. Allan Matthews had confirmed that we had a meeting set up at 11am and all key suppliers would be there along with himself and Martin Kirkbride. I had completed the presentation and we were all set to engage with them in a positive fashion.

Everyone was pumped up and I had a good feeling about all of this.

I wrote some actions on the flip chart with owners and time scales:

Actions	Who	When
1. Update directors on industrial action yesterday	Brian/Ralph	Today early
2. Gain agreement on using temporary crew	Mal/Sarah	Today early
3. Gain agreement on rescinding the old rules	Brian/Ralph	Today early
4. Give presentation to suppliers	Ralph/Allan	11am
5. Create temporary crew and communicate	Mal/Sarah	Today
6. Create training plan	Mal/Sarah	Today
7. Finish off planning rules and communicate	Robert	Today late
8. Communicate to all staff once we have agreement	Brian/Ralph	Today late

They were all taking notes as I looked around and asked "Are you all in agreement with the actions? Any questions?"

They were all nodding, so I said "Okay, let's get to it. Brian can you stay for a moment and we will work out what we need to do with the directors? Mal and Sarah when we have a time for seeing the directors, we'll give you a shout to come and join us. Brian and I will support you in that meeting. Okay?"

Brian stayed behind and said "This is all going really well, Ralph. We are challenging lots of old ways of working and it is refreshing to see everyone getting behind what we are doing, even the guys who walked out yesterday seem really positive about things this morning so it looks like we are heading in the right direction".

"That's good news. Do you have any thoughts on how we raise this with the directors?"

"They already know about most of it Ralph. There is not much that goes on in here that Leon doesn't get to know about. I think we should give them a verbal briefing about what happened and where we are up to now. Then we can get Mal and Sarah involved in the reasoning and numbers on the temporary crew and we can talk about the need to rescind the old rules. I know that Paul Howard gave out the old rules in writing but I think that if we keep focused on the positives rather than the negatives we should be able to get agreement from Martin and Leon very quickly and Paul will not argue with that".

"Do have to prepare a few slides?"

"No need. This should be a pretty quick meeting. Shall we call Leon now?"

"Let's do it"

Brian called Leon on the office phone and put it on speaker. Leon answered after a couple of rings and said "Hello Ralph, what can I do for you?"

"It's Brian here, Leon. Ralph and I are in his office and we have you on speaker".

"Ah, good morning to you both".

Brian continued "Leon, we would like to come and brief you on what happened yesterday on the walk out and also where we are on the removal of the WIP and what it means to the business. We would like to bring along Mal and Sarah as they have some numbers on that element and we would also like to have Paul Howard and Martin Kirkbride at the meeting. It will only take 15 to 20 minutes, so when is a good time to do this?"

"Just a second Brian, let me check my diary. Looks like I am free at 9:30 so let me call Paul and Martin and see if they can make that time. I'll come back to you shortly".

"Thanks Leon" said Brian.

I said to Brian "I will have to get used to this. When I started here, I wasn't expecting to be able to call the CEO and get to see him at the drop of a hat".

Brian replied "It's always been that way, Ralph. Leon likes to know what is going on and he genuinely has an open door policy when he is not doing his 90 minute power blocks. He makes himself available whenever he can and he generally doesn't attend a lot of meetings so his diary is relatively uncluttered most of the time".

"Well, I am not sure if it is normal in other companies, but I sure am glad that it applies here".

Just then the phone rang and Brian picked up "Yes Leon. Okay 9:30 it is, we'll be there".

Brian put the phone down and said "We are all set for 9:30 in Leon's office. Paul and Martin will be there as well. I will get Mal and Sarah organised to meet us there. Is there anything else to cover right now?"

"I don't think so Brian, see you there at 9:30". With that, Brian got up to leave.

When I was on my own again I decided to shoot a copy of the supplier presentation to Martin and Allan to get their comments. I was pretty sure that it would be okay, as the message was short and very positive. Nonetheless, I wanted to be sure that we were all on the same page – best to be safe.

When I had done that I started to write a few notes of the items we needed to cover with Leon and the other directors at our meeting this morning. I wanted to make sure that we covered all of the salient points.

At 9:25 Brian, Mal and Sarah all trooped into my office. They were all looking upbeat, so I asked "Are we all set for the meeting with the directors?"

Mal said "We have prepared a short handout rather than doing slides as we feel we can get our message across very simply and quickly by doing that. The numbers are so compelling that we don't think we'll get any push back on this".

"That sounds good, can I see the handout?"

Mal passed me a single sheet and we briefly discussed the points that were being made. I agreed with him that it did look like a very compelling case and I was happy with what was on there. I asked "So who is going to present the numbers?"

Sarah piped up "I have asked Mal if I can do it. I have never been in this situation before and I would like to get my feet wet".

"Good for you, Sarah" I said, "I think that will be a good move for you. It will lift your profile in the business and show you in a good light".

Mal said mischievously "Yeah, the directors are all suckers for a pretty face, so I figured it had better be Sarah because I certainly don't qualify!"

We all laughed and Sarah punched him playfully on the shoulder. I liked this team.

Brian said "Okay, time to go".

When we got there the door was open. We walked in and they were sitting around Leon's table waiting for us. We all sat and Leon looked around and said "Who is going to kick us off?"

I said "I will do it Leon. I have some notes just to remind me what I need to cover so if you are agreeable I'll just go through them from the top?"

"Fire away, Ralph" said Leon.

So I started my briefing. I gave them all a rundown on what had happened yesterday with the walk out situation. Brian chipped in and helped me out with some of the detail but they all got the gist of it pretty quickly. Leon said "Seems like you averted a potentially volatile situation very well between you, so well done. What sparked it off in the first place?"

I replied "We had spoken with Tommy Sherwin about the temporary crew to get rid of the WIP, and Tommy volunteered to go and speak to the people that were going to be affected. Next thing we knew, it had all kicked off".

Leon looked thoughtful and said "I don't think for a minute that Tommy would have done anything to inflame the situation, so I'm guessing it was one or two hot heads that created the situation?"

Brian responded "That's our view. Tommy was genuinely trying to help. I think it would have kicked off no matter who was delivering the message".

"And how is all looking this morning?" Leon asked.

"Good as gold" said Brian.

"Fantastic, then let's move on".

I said "Mal and Sarah have been working on the temporary crew that we would like to put together to get rid of the WIP in Final Assembly. Sarah has a few numbers that she would like to show you". I nodded to Sarah and she handed out the sheets to everyone.

She was a little red in the face as I guessed she had never had to do this before but she bravely started to describe the rationale behind the temporary crew and then went on to show the numbers and how it made lots of sense to make a move in this area.

Martin was asking all kinds of positive questions, as was Leon. Paul Howard did not say anything until she had come to the end. Then he said "So am I understanding this correctly Sarah? You are proposing that we take people out of chassis build and the body shop and use them to form a temporary crew to get rid of the WIP in Final Assembly?"

Sarah looked right at him as though she had been primed for this question and said "That is exactly what I am proposing Paul. The cost to the business is minimal and the benefits are massive. Do you have something else in mind?"

Now it was time for Paul to look a little flustered. He said "Quite the opposite Sarah, I think it is a great idea. But I have been thinking of something that might be a potential obstacle. Some time ago I gave instructions that the chassis shop and the body shop should not stop producing even though the parts were not fully available. I can see now that this might have contributed to our current situation. I will be happy to give them all instructions to follow your plan".

We were all stunned at this statement. Paul Howard was admitting in front of us and the other directors that he was in the wrong to do what he had done and was prepared to back us by giving new instructions.

I think that privately Leon had already twigged what was going on and he said "Thank you for your support of the team, Paul. I am happy to proceed with this, so let's make it happen. My only concern is that the people are trained properly and that quality is not compromised".

Mal spoke up "Leon I am taking responsibility for those elements personally so that I can be sure things are done right".

Leon looked pleased with this and said "That is good enough for me, Mal. What else have we got to cover?"

I took over once again and explained the new planning rules to them all and they all agreed with this. I then explained what we were doing with the key suppliers later today and to my surprise Martin Kirkbride took over the conversation and explained to Leon and Paul that he was fully behind the initiative and that he was going to be at the presentation to give us visible support in front of the suppliers.

Leon was looking pleased again. He said "You guys are doing some amazing stuff. You have my full support on this and if you need to wheel me in at any time just give me a call. I am happy to help".

We all breathed a collective sigh of relief and started to get ready to leave when Leon said "Ralph, could you and Brian stay behind for one minute please?"

When the room was clear Leon sat on the edge of his desk and looked right at me. His eyes started to close in the owl like way that he had, and he said very quietly "I think that you guys have done some great stuff over the last couple of weeks but there is one thing that I will not tolerate" and he opened his eyes again. The way he did that was very disconcerting.

He looked directly at me and said "Ralph, when you came to see me the other day you knew that Paul Howard had contributed to this situation and you chose to keep it from me. And you, Brian, you also knew and did not tell me either".

I knew I had been caught out and I could not argue the point. I said "Leon you are right. I did know about it and I thought that rather than point the finger at Paul I would focus on the issues. In retrospect, perhaps that was the wrong choice. I should have asked you for your advice".

"If you had done that, I would not be as angry as I am today. Do not keep anything of substance from me ever again. And Brian, you should have known better than to go along with it".

Brian looked contrite and said "Sorry Leon, it won't happen again".

"Okay. Keep me in the loop on the progress you are making and good luck with it. And remember I need people around me that I can trust implicitly without playing any dumb games. Agreed?"

"Yes Leon" we both said together.

We scooted out of the office and on the way back Brian said to me "We got off lightly there, you know".

"Really? It felt pretty crappy when he was telling us off".

"I have seen him rip people to shreds for doing less than we did. Believe me, we got off lightly".

As we walked past Paul Howard's office he caught sight of us through the open door and called us in. We looked at each other apprehensively.

"Come on in guys, let me have 5 minutes".

We went in and sat at his table and he came over and joined us.

He said "I would just like to thank you two for not dumping me in it with Leon".

I was astonished.

"Paul we had no intention of doing that. We just want to get a great result for the business and we are not interested in scoring points" I replied.

"I know that now Ralph, and I want to say that you have my full support going forward. The way you handled the situation yesterday and the fact that you protected me even though you knew I had contributed to the current situation means that I can trust you. The least I can do is to support you, so if there is anything I can do to help, just let me know and it will be done".

This was a day full of surprises.

Brian said "Leon just chewed us both out for not telling him the full story, so in future we will have to be more open and up front with him".

"That's fine with me. I don't have any more skeletons in my closet".

"Thanks Paul, we appreciate your support" said Brian, and we got up to leave.

This was even better than we could have hoped for. Paul Howard was probably the one guy in the whole business who could get things done quickly, and with his support we were very well placed.

When we got back to my office I said to Brian "This really is a strange day. We get chewed out by Leon and get a pledge of support from Paul Howard".

Brian was sanguine, he said "I take every win whenever I can get it. Leon will be okay. Paul has come down on the right side at last and we can now use him to get things moving. I am really pleased with where we have got to this morning".

I was really pleased too. I looked at my watch and it was 10:40. I said to Brian "I am going to prepare for the meeting with the suppliers. I'll catch you later".

Brian got up and left me to it.

I then checked my emails to see if there was a response from Allan or Martin and there was an email from each of them. I opened the one from Allan first. He was saying that he agreed with the presentation but it maybe needed a little more of what was in it for the suppliers. I opened the one from Martin and he virtually said the same thing. I was wondering about that when I noticed the time. I had to get over to the meeting room in time for the presentation.

On the way over there I was thinking about what else I could offer the suppliers to get behind our initiative but nothing was springing to my mind.

When I got to the meeting room, Allan was already there setting things up. There was a projector shining on to the wall with the presentation open on the front page. Allan was on the ball. There was a white board with markers on the long wall and a flip chart with markers in the corner, so it looked like we were in good shape. I asked Allan if all of the suppliers were coming and he said that they had all accepted and most of them were sending a very senior person to attend. They were clearly all taking it seriously.

Just then Martin came in, so we had a quick chat about what else we could offer the suppliers as an incentive. I had been thinking about this for quite a while and I suggested that perhaps we could invite them to be a part of our improvement effort by contributing to our improvement teams and we could do the same for them to help them to improve. That way we could create a better working relationship and build trust between us. They both liked that, so I made a note to add it to the end of the presentation.

Then the suppliers started to arrive. One of the girls in reception was showing them into the meeting room and we began the round of introductions and handshakes. Most of them knew Allan even if it was only from phone calls, but none of them knew me or Martin.

There were twelve people from our suppliers. Out of that, eight of them had the title of director and the rest were senior managers, so it was a high powered meeting.

When they were all settled Allan called the meeting to order and asked us all to briefly introduce ourselves to the group. This took up the first 10 minutes and served to break the ice somewhat. Then Allan handed over to me and I started my presentation.

I took them through the slides at a steady pace and I told them exactly what the state of play was at Millikan and where we were up to in terms of our improvement plans. I also told them what we would like from them and what it would allow us to do. I held nothing back and I watched them the whole time. Finally I invited them all to be part of our improvement journey and actually attend our improvement events, and said that we would do the same for them if they wanted. Right at the very end I asked them for their support so that we could get this plan enacted quickly.

Before I sat down, Martin Kirkbride stood up and said "Thank you Ralph, that was an excellent presentation. Before we get into the questions, I just wanted to add a few words of my own".

He looked around the room slowly as if he was sizing up all of the players in the room and he said "I have been in finance for 30 years and I have seen it all. I can honestly say that the last 3 years have been some of the most challenging ones in my career but also some of the most rewarding. Millikan are changing the car industry and I am very proud to be a part of it. But we've managed to get ourselves into this precarious position, and I can tell you that it has tested us all. Since Ralph has arrived we have started to see the light again. He has helped us to see what was hidden in plain sight. I firmly believe that we now have the road map identified which will allow us to get Millikan back into the black very quickly, but we cannot do this without your support. You and your teams are critical to our future. I know that we have not been the best payer over the last couple of years because, as you have seen this morning, we have had all our cash tied up in WIP. That is about to change in a big way. As a main Board Director of the business I am here to add my full support to the plan that Ralph has outlined to you today and I am now asking you all for your full and continued support to get Millikan and all of your companies back on to the right footing. Thank you all".

I had never heard Martin speak in public before and I did not have him pegged as an orator but boy was I wrong. His words were very well received and he got a round of applause as he sat down. Then Allan stood up and said "Okay, you have all heard what Ralph has to say and also the strong words of support from Martin. Are there any questions?"

One of the managing directors in the room said "Firstly Allan I would like to thank you for the invitation to come here today. I must confess that I was more than a little sceptical about what to expect, but I have been very pleasantly surprised. I did not expect you to tell us the extent of your current position and having heard what you have to say

I can understand why you have struggled for the last couple of years. I can also see that you now have a plan in place and how we can play our part in that plan. I like all of that and I accept it. However, can you give us any assurances that if we do agree to help you that, firstly, we will be paid the arrears that are past due; and secondly, that we will get paid promptly for the work that we are about to commit to your business?"

Martin Kirkbride stood up once again and he said "Allan let me take that one. It is a very fair question and I think that I can answer it honestly. If we manage to get rid of the WIP that is currently eating all of our cash it will put around £105m into our coffers over the next few weeks. That will come to us before we release the vehicles as they have to be paid in full before they are shipped. That will enable us to pay all of our past due accounts to your companies without fail and will also allow us to pay for the work that you are about to do on our behalf. It will turn the business around very quickly. Going forward, with the plan that Ralph and the team are working on, we will not allow the WIP to grow and consume our cash like it has done in the past. We will have early warning mechanisms in place to alert us to impending danger and allow us to react accordingly. I cannot promise all plain sailing as I don't have my crystal ball handy – but I can say that we will be working with you to ensure that we do not get into this condition again. Millikan is potentially a very profitable business and by redesigning our process we will be a very efficient business that is able to produce at a higher rate and at a lower cost. I can only see the future getting better for us all".

Martin had done it again. He was stealing the show and doing a damn good job of it.

There were quite a few more questions from the other attendees but nothing too dramatic, and at the end of it we had an agreement in principle that they would all support us by supplying the key missing parts that we needed over the next 4-6 weeks. This would enable us to finish the bulk of the cars in WIP. It was a fantastic result.

After all of the visitors had gone I thanked Martin and Allan for their support. They were both magnanimous and said that it was me who had got us to this point and they were happy to do their part. This was turning out to be a red letter day in many respects.

Now I just had to start working on the new process and we would be in good shape!

When I got back to my room my stuff was missing and I gave Brian a call. He said that he had found me a new office and he had got me installed already. I got to his office and he was there talking to Mal and Sarah. I gave them a rundown on what had happened with the key suppliers and they were all delighted with the outcome. Then Brian said "Come and have a look at your new office".

I followed him out of the door and along the corridor almost to the shop floor. He opened the last door on the right and went in. I followed him in and was pleased to find myself in an office that could have been purpose designed for me and what I had to do. It had two desks back to back just inside the door and a big meeting table in the middle of the room. There were windows running down one wall which looked out into the factory, which was very handy. It had a projector, a huge white board along one wall and a flip chart. It looked like I was all set. Brian said "This used to be our morning meeting room but we have it in a much bigger place now. We have got yours and Sarah's stuff all plugged in and ready to go".

I said "Brian, you are a star. Thank you very much for this".

"No worries, Ralph. All part of the service and it gets you so much closer to the action!"

I was very pleased with this new room. It was close to Brian, Mal, Tommy, and the shop floor. It had everything I needed and it was nice to have my own room. I felt like I was really becoming part of the company.

I said to Brian "It looks like we have the go-ahead on all of the items we created on our action list this morning. Should we get the team back together before we go home to have a quick round up?"

"Sounds like a good plan, Ralph. I will get them all to come to your new room".

The team started to wander in and a few minutes later I gave them all a quick rundown of what had happened at the meeting with the suppliers. We basked in the warm afterglow for a few moments before I called them back to reality. I said "This is a great result and it now means we have two things to do. One is to finalise the work that we need to put in place to get the WIP down to a manageable level. Secondly, we need to start working on the new process for when the WIP is under control. That is a lot of work and we need to start right now".

I asked Robert if he had worked out the new planning rules fully and got the IT support that he needed. He said "It is all done Ralph. I have briefed the whole planning team on what they need to do. The new parts start arriving tomorrow and Paul Howard has just issued a memo to all staff to say that the previous instructions are now rescinded and that we must all now follow the new planning rules to get rid of the WIP. We just need the temporary team in place and we are good to go".

"That sounds great, Robert. We are making really fast progress now" I responded.

Mal said "I am working on the temporary team now. The volunteer forms are all in place and we are getting a good take up from all areas".

"Thanks Mal" I replied

"What we need to do now is to follow through on all of this stuff and get the WIP moving through the process and out of the door as quickly as we possibly can. Robert, can you provide us with an update every morning to show how much WIP we have moved out?"

"Yes Ralph, that's easy for us to do".

"Great. Now, does anyone have any thoughts on how to get started designing the new process?"

Brian stood up and went to the flip chart. He said "I have been thinking about this a lot, and with the insights you've given us I think that there is a way to do it that will get us a much better result".

We were all intrigued, and Sarah said "Sounds very encouraging Brian, what do you have in mind?"

Brian looked a little sheepish and said "This is hard for me in lots of ways, because I designed most of the original process myself. But when I take a good, hard look at it there are opportunities at every step that can make it better".

Brian continued, "We have a number of distinct production areas that all form one large string of events. We build every car as we go along and we don't really make very many sub-assemblies. This is a massive opportunity. Also, we have never balanced the whole end to end process or really designed the buffers to get the best result. This is also an opportunity. We have never tried to approximate an assembly line as we have always been focused on the hand-built element, which is fine but it limits your thinking and does not allow you to see other possibilities. All of this got me thinking about how we could do things differently, and I think I know how. If we set up the production process to mimic an assembly line, it makes you think about the work content and the beat rate of every process. So if we look at each element as if it is critically attached to its neighbour on either side, we can start to design a process that is much more like a flow than a series of separate departments".

We all sat for a moment to take this in. Brian had clearly been giving this a lot of thought. Mal said "I think I follow all of that Brian, but what does it mean in practical terms? What do we have to do to mimic the assembly line?"

"I think we have to lay it all out as it currently exists and break each area down into a TAKT[2] time so that we can get a beat rate going through the whole process. We have to work out the content to match or exceed the TAKT time and assume that all parts are available in the right place at the right time. We have to work out what size buffers we need in between processes and we have to assume that we cannot build WIP. If this was a true assembly line it would stop if we had no parts or if we had a breakdown. We have to create that same set of conditions".

Sarah chipped in and said "But what is TAKT time?"

Brian said "I have been reading up on this subject for a while and I can give you an example. If we have a customer demand of 100 vehicles per week and we work a single 8 hour shift for 5 days each week this will give us 40 working hours per week. That means we have to complete 2.5 finished cars or their equivalent every hour to meet the customer demand or one car every 24 minutes, so 24 minutes becomes our TAKT time. It also means that if we had a moving assembly line, it would index forward every 24 minutes and all work required in that part of the process would need to be completed to allow the line to move forward. We need to build in some wiggle room and time to fill the buffers so we would target a slightly better time than that but it gives us a basic principle to work with".

We were all buzzing. Brian had just given us the next Silver Bullet that we needed to unlock this puzzle.

There was lots of excited murmuring in the room and Brian said "However, I'm not an expert at this. I was hoping that Ralph could help us with the details".

---

[2] **Takt time** is the maximum amount of **time** in which a product needs to be produced in order to satisfy customer demand. The term comes from the German word "**takt**," which means "pulse".

This was my cue to jump in and agree a way forward. I said "As it happens I do know something about TAKT time and how it works. Think of it as a heartbeat that keeps on pumping at the same rate the whole time. The way we should approach this is to break the whole process into 24 minute blocks. This will give us the number of work stations we need. As we move through the process we can build in some additional capacity so that if we have any stoppages or breakdowns we can catch up what we have lost. I think that this is a great thing to work on as a team and break it up into manageable pieces so that we can get it sorted really quickly".

Brian perked up and said "That sounds like a great idea. Shall we allocate areas to the team and see how we get on?"

"Sounds like a plan to me, Brian" I replied.

We all got into a huddle and sketched out the process in block diagrams and we allocated areas as Brian had suggested. Sarah was allocated chassis build and body shop, I took paint and rework, Mal took electrical and motor installation, Brian took trim and final assembly, and Robert took final inspection and test.

I stood up and said "Guys, I suggest that we do this in a particular way. We should get the SOPs (Standard Operating Procedures) that already exist and use them as the basis of what we are trying to do. We should sit with the supervisor and other key staff in the area and let them know what we are trying to achieve. We should map out the current process in that area and then look at ways we can get all operations into a 24 minute time slot. If there are two shifts in a certain area then the time slot will be 48 minutes, and we will need to have a buffer between that area and the next one to guarantee the supply line. Do you all follow what I am saying?"

Robert was looking thoughtful and he said "I think so Ralph, but I have never done this before and I don't know much about process mapping".

I was thinking the same thing myself but this was not the time to be shy. I said "Robert, none of us are experts in every process and we will need to rely on the local expertise to get this right. If we approach it with an open mind and the conviction in our hearts that we will find a way then we will succeed. Use the expertise wherever you find it and don't be afraid to ask questions, no matter how basic or dumb they might seem to you. Nobody will expect you to be an expert, so don't try to be one. Just work with the guys in the area, let them know that you need their help and I am pretty sure they will give it"

Mal was nodding, he said "Ralph is right. We are all going into this with different levels of knowledge and experience. The guys at the sharp end on the shop floor will be the real experts. Give them the respect that they deserve and you'll get what you need".

Sarah was also looking a bit apprehensive. She said "I was thinking exactly the same thing but I was just going to bat my eyelashes, show a bit of cleavage and play the damsel in distress. I find it works for me".

Robert roared with laughter and said "I don't think that approach will work for me Sarah, but I can give it a try!"

We all laughed out loud and the atmosphere became much more relaxed again.

Brian brought us back to order. He said "We should aim to get all departments on to the same shift pattern with the same TAKT time if we possibly can. Think about doubling up and doing some creative stuff. There are a number of ways to do that so when you talk to the guys in areas with two shifts, ask them how we can get back to a single shift without losing any people. Also we should be looking to build as many sub-assemblies offline as we can. That way, we're not actually building, we're assembling, which should make things a lot quicker".

This got us all buzzing and we were ready to hit the road. I said "Grab a blank pad and just sketch it all by hand when you are talking to the guys. Nothing fancy just simple block diagrams are fine. Let's reconvene back here at 4:30 and see how we are all getting on". With that we all set off to our allocated areas and got stuck into the next part of our journey.

At 4:30 we all came back to my office with a whole bunch of notes in our hands. I asked Sarah to give us a quick rundown on what she had achieved with the guys in chassis build. She showed us all the diagrams and notes she had written and said "I sat down with the chassis build supervisor and, believe it or not, Davey Maguire joined us. We really got to grips with this process mapping. The process in the chassis build area does not lend itself exactly to a 24 minute TAKT time, but with a bit of jigging around we managed to get it done. The guys will have to build some new fixtures and rearrange the work stations a bit, but they reckon it can be done in one night with the right guys on the job".

Mal said "Outstanding. That means we can use that as a foundation to build on for the rest of the process. What next, Ralph?"

"Well assuming that we can get the area rearranged as Sarah is suggesting, we need to redo the SOP documents and train all staff in the area to do their part of the process. Will it mean any additional staff?"

Sarah looked thoughtful and said "It actually means we can do it with less staff. We will be able to release two people from the chassis build area into other parts of the process. We don't have any temporary staff there, so simply letting them go is not an option".

Brian said "That's good, Sarah. Did you look into building any sub-assemblies offline?"

Sarah replied "There is very little we can do in that regard Brian as there are not a lot of chassis parts that lend themselves to being assembled offline. We did agree that a supply area could be set up in one corner that would make all of the braces and gussets that they need on the line rather than the welders making their own".

"That's perfect" said Brian. I could tell that he was pleased with the progress we were making.

I called them to order and said "Guys we have a lot to do in the next few days so let's call it a day. We still have to rollout the WIP removal process and make that work, so let's make sure that's a success and then we can carry on with this exercise. I am really pleased with where we have got to so far".

They were all smiling and Mal said "I have a ton of work to do tomorrow, so I will be reporting on my progress in a few days. I am really looking forward to the next couple of weeks".

And with that we broke up for the day and started to head off home.

Brian stayed behind and said to me "Ralph, I can hardly believe how far we have come in such a short time. This is going to be a blast for all of us".

"You're dead right, Brian. I can hardly believe it myself. Now that we have got some momentum we should really start to roll. We need to get the WIP moving out to generate the cash and then we can get lots of other stuff done".

Brian said "Yes, and I am looking forward to making all of these changes happen. I have never seen myself as being able to change the future of a business. I guess I never really thought at those levels before, but I can see a whole new way of managing and looking at the world now, and I have you to thank for that".

"No thanks required Brian. We are all a team and contributing in our own different ways, and when that happens the end result is greater than the sum of the parts. I'm looking forward to the rest of this journey. Now let's go home before I start bawling!"

We both laughed together and Brian gave me a playful punch on the shoulder. He was a top performer and to get this kind of reaction from him was something special for me.

I drove home in great spirits that night and when I opened the front door there was a letter addressed to me sitting on the hall table. I tore it open and it was my first pay check from Millikan. When I saw the number on the check I almost jumped with joy. This was the start of my own career turnaround and I meant to make the best of it. I shouted out to Maricel and then I realised that the house was eerily quiet. I walked from room to room to see where she was but she was not at home. I called her cell phone to see where she was but it went straight to voice mail. I was wondering what to do next when my phone buzzed. I looked down and I had a text message from Maricel's mother. It said "Ralph, Maricel is staying with me for a few days. She is not well and she does not need any more stress. She will call you in the next few days".

I was floored by this. I thought that we had gotten over the worst of this bad patch and we were looking forward to a brighter future, but it looked like I was wrong. I tried to call her mother but it went to voice mail also. Looks like I was going to be on my own for a while. There was something I didn't need right now. I thought that getting my first pay check was going to be a happy occasion. How wrong could I be?

F IS FOR FINE TUNE:
RALPH'S REFLECTIONS

After such a crazy week I wrote down my learning points in my journal:

This week I had learned that selecting an option is sometimes easy and sometimes not so easy. The important thing was to secure consensus from the team and gain commitment to the direction of travel. These are the key issues. In this instance the option was kind of chosen for us, and this is what happens sometimes. The important thing was that we were all in agreement that it was the right thing to do at this time in the business and in our transformation project. I had also learned that there will be times when you need to take a detour. This is not a bad thing, as long as you remember that communication is the key to making everything work. Do not assume that other people will know what you know and think the same way that you do. There may be aggressive reactions to your proposals that you need to deal with and sometimes you will have to 'earn your spurs' and defend your ideas to people who are not fully bought-in, like I had to do when the staff walked out.

Support can come from the most unexpected people and areas of the business, so don't overlook talent that may be right in front of you. One of the surprises for me was that suppliers can be your biggest allies if you treat them correctly. That certainly seemed to be the case in this situation. Also when you have taken a detour it is critical that you communicate the reasons well and keep people in the loop so that there are no misunderstandings.

I had also learned that getting back on track after a detour is very important to getting the best result possible and for keeping people focused. Some people will be outside of their comfort zones and will need plenty of support, so be prepared to give it where necessary. The results when you get an energised team can come very quickly and be very positive, so you need to ride the wave when you get the opportunity.

Personal Life

This had been a big learning week for me not only in how to apply the 7 Steps to Profit in difficult circumstances but also in how to manage the change process and also in how to calm an angry mob! The roller coaster ride for me this week was pretty spectacular and in some ways I was glad that I had come through this week relatively unscathed work-wise. It was not great, having to get up in front of the striking workforce, but I did it and I am glad that I did it. I also got chewed out by Leon, and whilst it was a gentle mauling compared to what it could have been, it was nerve-wracking all the same. He could end my consulting career before it had really begun. I also learned a bit more about human nature. The episode with Paul Howard still surprises me. He changed his attitude completely and it was down to the fact that we protected him and kept him out of the firing line with Leon. He respected that and, fair play to the guy, he did the right thing and offered his full support.

My personal life was taking a strange turn, however. Maricel had decided to take off and stay with her mother and would not answer her phone. That was a big surprise. I know that things had been a bit tense just lately and I know that she will be feeling unwell at the start of her pregnancy, but I would have expected her to stick around so that we could enjoy the journey together. I will call her tomorrow or go round to her mother's house and see if I can speak to her and sort things out. I really want my marriage to be a wonderful experience for both of us and to bring our baby into the world in a happy and safe environment with two loving parents. It looks like that will take some working out. Creating magic moments like the dinner and flowers is one thing, but consistently being there for Maricel is what it will take in the long term.

I had lost more weight this week and I had just started to sneak in a five minute meditation here and there and the seven minute workout was starting to show on my upper and lower body. Excellent stuff.

> To get the free in-depth video tutorial on this step of
> 7 Steps to Profit go to **www.90daystoprofit.co.uk/bonus**

7 STEPS TO PROFIT

5 Implement & Test
4 Fine Tune
3 Opportunities
2 Review
1 Problems

CHAPTER FIVE

I IS FOR IMPLEMENT & TEST

SAM'S SESSION 5

I was not in a good mood when I turned up for my class on Saturday morning. Sam sensed that there was something amiss, and as there were others already there he asked me to walk with him outside for a moment. When we were outside he said "So tell me – what's eating you this morning, Ralph?"

"Maricel has gone to live with her mother for a few days" I replied gloomily.

"Well, I'm sure she just needs a little space. Can I ask what brought this on, or is it too personal?"

"It's been coming for a while. When I lost my job we struggled for a long time to make ends meet and she was the breadwinner. Then I took on this course without any idea how I was going to pay for it. I was not going to get paid for two months from Millikan and the bills kept rolling in. I guess things just got on top of her and she couldn't handle the stress in her condition".

"Her condition?"

"She's expecting our first child".

"That's great news, congratulations. But I think we need a longer chat about this. Can you stay behind after the session this morning?"

"I have nothing else to do, so why not?" I replied gloomily again.

"Let's focus on the session for now and we can talk later" he said, and we went back inside.

We started as normal with an update on what we were all doing. I was turning into a bit of a celebrity with my high profile client and the apparent progress we were making, and they were all asking questions. It got me into a better mood, if only for a little while.

Sam said "Great work, Ralph. Seems like you are making fantastic progress. Now what is step 5?"

We had all got the gist of this by now and we knew instinctively that we had to start to put the solution into actual practice – to Implement and Test. The slant that Sam put on it was to always try to run a pilot program first. This was interesting, because in a way we had already done this by selecting the Final Assembly area to start getting through the WIP. We had done the right thing without even realising it. I must be getting better at this consultancy lark, I thought to myself. If it was not possible for any reason to run a pilot, then we should roll it out across the business but stress test it first. By this he meant that we should look at what the possible outcomes could be and assign probabilities to each one to determine the level of risk we were about to take on.

"In the SAS we would train drills about 95% of the time, so when it came to actually doing something on a mission we would know what to do on autopilot" Sam said. He added that when it came to specific missions they would always do a dry run many times until it was 100% perfect. He reminded us of the bouncing bombs story of World War 2. There were many practice runs on local dams and reservoirs before they got the technique just right. They did not set off on the mission until they had convinced themselves that it was achievable and that they had taken out as much of the risk as possible. That was exactly what we were doing by removing the WIP from the current process.

The session was over very quickly and the guys started to thin out. Sam collared me and took me over to the corner of the room to a small table with a couple of chairs. We sat opposite each other and he said "Okay Ralph, you want to talk about all this?"

I must confess I was still not feeling great, but I started to tell him what had happened over the last few weeks. After I got him up-to-date, he said "So, you finally got your first pay packet and Maricel decides she has had enough and takes off to stay with her mother?"

"Well, to be fair, it was not going great for a long time before that and she didn't know what was in the envelope. She has been really stressed for a few months and I was not making things any better by working long hours and probably not spending enough time with her when she was feeling at a very low ebb. The pregnancy won't be helping with her mood and I am now in a spot where I had never thought I would be. That has happened to me a lot in recent times. I never expected to be fired, I never expected it would be so hard to find a new job, I never expected to be scratching to pay my bills, I never expected to be a father so soon, and I never expected Maricel to leave me like this. Apart from all that I am in fine shape" I said, and managed half a smile.

Sam said "I think what I am hearing now is a bit of self-pity, which is not attractive. If I were in your shoes I would be planning how to get her back home double-quick and make her life with you a wonderful and joyous place to be. Do you believe that you can do that? As Henry Ford said: 'Whether you think you can, or whether you think you can´t, you're right'. It's your choice, so what is it going to be?"

"I am going to get her back home double-quick and start making her life with me a wonderful and joyous place to be" I said, using the same phrasing as Sam had a moment ago.

He laughed and said "That's the spirit, Ralph. Now go and do it!"

Running a Pilot Program

I had tried to speak to Maricel, but she was still not having any of it, so I had spent my day catching up on my notes and doing some exercises to get my body into shape. My morning routine now consisted of the following: seven or eight hours of hours sleep, five minutes of meditation, seven minutes of exercise, and a green smoothie. The more often I did this, the more perky I felt throughout the day.

On Monday morning I got into work at 8am as usual and got ready for an interesting week. I created my to-do list for the day and just as I was finishing, Brian came in. He said "Hi Ralph, what have we got in store this week?"

I put down my pen and stood up. I said "We have got a really busy week ahead of us Brian and I am not sure we can do it all but we are going to give it our best shot. We have to run the WIP project as a pilot program in the Final Assembly area and we need to make a really good job of it. It is all set up and Mal is doing the managing, but we need to support him to the max. Also we need to map out the rest of the process and make some decisions on how we are going to improve it to stop the build-up of WIP in future. How about we check in with Mal and see how he is getting on?"

"Okay, let's do that" he replied, and we set off for the Final Assembly area.

We went straight to the corner where the WIP cars were being finished and we found Mal in the thick of the action.

I shook his hand and said "Hi Mal, how are you getting on?"

He was smiling so I guessed it had got off to a good start. He said "It is going great Ralph. All of the parts that we were promised have arrived and we have several guys creating kits of parts for us. The guys doing the work are picking it up really well and we have finished two cars this morning already".

I was blown away. At this rate we would finish in half the estimated time. I asked him "So what is your new estimate for completion?"

"Too early to say right now, but it is not going to take 4 weeks. More like 3 weeks I would think, as we're doing the easiest ones first. Some of the later ones will be a little trickier".

I was happy with that and I asked Brian "So how do we go about tracking our progress with this?"

Brian was a step ahead as usual and he showed me a tally board set up on a flip chart in front of the WIP build area. It was a simple handwritten record of which cars were being completed, what the original ID had been, and what the new ID was going to be. It had the daily plan from Robert pinned to the top left hand corner to act as a guide for the sequencing.

This was simple and brilliant at the same time. I could hardly believe that something so simple could be so effective. It did not have to be fancy or computer-generated to be effective, it just had to work. That was very good KISS (Keep It Simple, Stupid!) learning for me.

I thanked Mal for his efforts, and Brian and I made our way back to my office.

When we got there I said "It looks like we are going to blitz our original estimate and get the money flowing back into the company bank account in double quick time. I think we need to check in with Robert to make sure we are able to keep track of all the changes and make sure that we are only working on the cars that we can finish, but on the face of it we are in really good shape".

Brian said "I agree, Ralph. I will pop up and see Robert shortly and then I will go and run the daily meeting. When I am done there, I'll come back down and we can agree next steps".

Off he went, and I sat down to look at the work that had been done by the team at the end of last week. The process was largely mapped out and we were starting to get it split into blocks of 24 minutes to establish the TAKT time in every area. The difficult bits would be framing, paint, and Final Assembly. As I was thinking about this, Martin Kirkbride walked in. I was surprised, as he had never come to see me before. I jumped up and said "Good morning Martin, how can I help you?" And I motioned for him to sit at my meeting table.

He sat and looked at me thoughtfully. He said "Ralph, I have some good news and some bad news. Which would you like first?"

I wasn't sure that he was being serious but then I looked at his eyes and I could see that he was deadly serious.

I said "You choose, Martin".

So he looked at me again and said "We are not going to create a new process. That is the bad news, as I know how hard you and the team have worked to get to this point. The good news is that we are going to refine and perfect the process that you have created to manage and control the WIP. We are going to make people multi-skilled, flexible, and mobile so that they can work anywhere. We will take the work that Robert has done so far and we will figure out what else needs to be done to systematise it and we will run with that for another 18 months until we bring out the next model. We figured that it is not going to be worth re-engineering the whole process now when instead we can manage it tightly, make tons of money in the meantime, and then when we are ready to launch the new model we will rejig the whole process at that point".

I was floored and at first I did not know what to say. Martin saw my confusion and said softly "Ralph, this is not a reflection on anything that you or the rest of the team have done. Quite the opposite we are delighted with everything that you have done. We would like you to stay on and finish the WIP project. We will work out what you have added to the business in terms of enterprise value and we will pay you a substantial bonus. When we are ready to redesign the new process we will call you to come and do it for us and we will give you the best reference you are ever likely to get".

I mentally gave my head a shake and said "What brought this on, Martin? On Friday we were all set to go ahead and I have got the whole team working on the new process".

Martin looked at me in his careworn way and said "These things happen in business. We were getting enormous pressure from the banks and we could see a way to make good on all of our promises in a very short time without going to the time, trouble and expense of redesigning a new process. It was Leon who made the decision and I can tell you from first-hand experience that when he makes up his mind it stays made up".

I was reading between the lines and it made me think that Martin did not fully agree with that decision and he had somehow drawn the short straw to come and tell me the news. I may have been wrong, but that is how it came across to me.

I said "So what would you like me to do now, Martin?"

He stood up and said "I would like you to get the whole team together and I will tell them what is going on".

I grabbed my iPhone and texted the WhatsApp group I had created with the team and asked them to meet me in my office.

Twenty minutes later we were all assembled in my office. Sarah had just come in and Brian had finished the morning meeting so the timing was perfect.

Martin brought us all to order and said "Guys, I have some news for you. There is no point sugarcoating it – the redesigning of the new process has been put on hold. All work on it will cease as of this morning. We are launching a new model in 18 months and we will redesign the new process to match the timing of that model launch. Clearly we will take all of the learning from the last few weeks and we will apply it to the new process and reassemble this team, including Ralph, to do it when the time comes. We love what this team has done so far and we want to capitalise on that teamwork and sense of purpose in the future. What we would like you all to do now is to focus on the WIP removal project in every part of the business, not just Final Assembly. We figure this might take another 4-6 weeks at the speed this team works and we will use the output from that work to take us through the next 18 months. It will allow us to work quickly and profitably and bring a lot of cash into the business. I would like to thank you for what you have done so far and encourage you not to lose heart. This has been a fantastic experience for us all, and this is just a twist in the road to a much brighter future. Are there any questions?"

The team started to murmur and Brian said "Martin this is a surprise given the level of support we have received so far. Is there anything we can do to change this decision and carry on with what we started?"

Brian was brave as usual and he had voiced what everyone else was thinking.

Martin said "My view is that the decision has been made and it will not be unmade. You are welcome to go and talk to Leon if that is what you want to do. On the other hand you have still got 6 weeks work left to get the WIP project finalised and working well in all parts of the factory. That is a lot of work in itself, and if you do it well it will make a massive contribution to the business. My advice would be to focus on that and do it to the very best of your ability".

I had gotten over my initial shock and I had my positive head back on. I got up in front of the group and said "Guys, this is a tough thing for Martin to come and tell us. I think we should listen to his advice and look upon this as an opportunity. There is still £150m worth of WIP in all parts of the business which we can liberate in the next 6 weeks. That is a huge influx of cash and a huge positive impact on the bottom line of the business. It will set the standard and tone for the next 18 months and when it comes time to redesign the process we will be well and truly ready for it with the groundwork we have already done. Let's give this our fullest attention and effort and make it a project that everyone will remember for the rest of their lives. It is not every day that you will get the opportunity to do this for any business, let alone one as big and as famous as Millikan. Let's go team, time to get things done!"

Martin shook my hand in gratitude, and the team all had their smiles back.

It was not what I expected this morning but I remembered what Sam had told me a couple of weeks ago. He said that this kind of thing happened all of the time and you just had to do whatever is required to get the best result for the business. When I first came to Millikan I thought it would be three months with a possibility to extend if it went well. Now I knew that there was an end date in sight and the terms of reference had changed, but I had been promised a substantial bonus and a fantastic reference from one of most well-known companies in the world. Life was not that bad, was it?

After Martin had left us I got the team around the meeting table and got them re-energised. Between us we worked out what we were going to do, and it was very similar to what we had just been doing. Instead of working out a completely new process with a consistent TAKT time we were now going to focus on keeping the WIP flowing in each area. It was a slightly different activity, but still engaging with the same people. Robert took over the conversation part way through as it was clear that he had already been doing some work on this. Once everyone understood their new brief they all headed back out on to the lines where they could start to do their new tasks.

At the end there was just myself and Brian and he said "Ralph, this is a strange day. I thought that this WIP reduction program was a temporary fix while we were looking at the whole process and now it looks like it has turned into the main project after all. Your handling of the situation just now with Martin was unbelievable. If someone had just come and taken my project off me I don't think I would have been as positive as you were. I think that you are going to have a fantastic career as a transformation consultant and I might just join you in that line of work".

I was blown away once more. I had no idea that this was coming and I had to stop for a moment and reflect on what Brian had just said. I looked at him and said "Brian, you are a star. I had no idea that this was coming. What do you have in mind?"

Brian looked thoughtful for a moment and said "This last few weeks have been the most exciting and fulfilling of my working life. I have done things that I never imagined doing. I have seen you in action and seen how you approach things and I really like it. If I could learn how to do it properly I would love to help other companies to achieve their goals as well".

I responded positively "Brian, I have also learnt a lot from you in this last few weeks. You are a natural communicator and you know what makes people tick. Those are valuable skills and if you decided to become a transformation consultant I would be more than happy to teach you what Sam Newton has been teaching me. Sam is the real expert and I am just learning, so if you wanted to take this forward I would advise you to sign up for one of Sam's courses".

Brian had a sparkle in his eye and he said "How about you and I joining forces and doing this together?"

It was the day for surprises alright. I said "That sounds like something we should discuss further, Brian. In the meantime how about we put all of our efforts into getting this one finished off and we can talk about what might happen next?"

"Sure thing Ralph – let's go and get it done" and he turned and left my office.

I was sitting there alone when the phone rang. I looked at the display and it was Leon. I picked up and said good morning to him. He replied in a bouncy tone "Morning Ralph. Martin said that he had given you the news about the process redesign and that you had taken it very positively and rallied the team around this new area of focus. I think I may have underestimated you Ralph. Come up and talk to me". So I set off for his office wondering what was in store for me next.

I got to his office and all 3 directors were sitting there which was a surprise. Martin and Paul were sitting at the meeting table and Leon was sitting at his desk. When I popped my head in Leon jumped up and said "Come in, Ralph", and he motioned for me to join Paul and Martin at the table. I sat down opposite Paul, leaving the seat at the head of the table for Leon. He joined us and said "Ralph, I know that you must have been disappointed to get the news this morning and we wanted to tell you something of what brought us to this decision. We also wanted to let you know that we have been mightily impressed with the work that you have done with the team so far. You have brought things out of them that we have not seen before and you are a natural leader. But first let me tell you about some of our thinking.

"I agree that the process we have is a bit of a mish-mash and a lot of that is due to my insistence on the hand-built promise to our customers. I hold my hand up and say that I take responsibility for that part. When we looked at what you and the team had done to free up the WIP, we knew that this would hugely boost the cash flow in the short term. Our challenge is to keep the business in that condition and that is the challenge that you have in the next few weeks – to drive the methodology for freeing up WIP into all parts of the process and give us the checks and balances to keep it under control. At this stage that will be more than enough for us to get to our next product launch. When we launch the new model we will do it in a new facility and with a state of the art automated process, so there is really no point in getting this process redesigned right now when everything will be superseded soon. I must be honest Ralph, when I asked Martin to go and tell you about our decision, we expected you to take it quite badly. We did not expect you to take it in such a positive way and to rally the team behind you to get the WIP project completed. We need people like you in this business, with a positive outlook and a 'can do' attitude, and we'd like to make you an offer".

I looked at him expectantly and said "Thank you Leon. I have really enjoyed these last few weeks at Millikan. What did you have in mind?"

"We know that you are just starting out on your career as a consultant and we all agree that you will make a success of your chosen career. To get you established we have 3 other businesses that we would like you to transform and we reckon that it will take you about 12 months to get all 3 of them back on their feet. When you have finished doing that, we want you to come back and work with the same team that you have put together here and design a completely new process for us. We are putting together a team of automation experts as we speak who can design the hardware and the Program Logic Controller systems and we would like you to be the leader of the whole team. We will keep you on contract at your current day rate for the next 2 years to get the new process fully bedded in. After that – you can go and conquer the world with our blessing".

I sat there with my mouth open for a few moments and then reality kicked in and I said "Leon, that is a fantastic offer and I can honestly say that this day is turning out to be one of the strangest days of my life so far. I have a couple of conditions that I would like you to consider. Firstly, when we have finished the WIP project I know that you have already said that you will look at a bonus for me and I am happy about that. I would also like you to consider a bonus for the team members as well. Secondly, when I go off and transform your other businesses I would like to take Brian with me. We'll work on them as a team and we'll come back to Millikan as a team. I would like you to treat it as a secondment and pay him the same daily rate that you are paying me. When we come back here, I would like us to agree the objectives and fully articulate what success looks like. When we have achieved those objectives we will shake hands and go our separate ways. It may take more or less than two years, so rather than working to a time scale I would prefer to work towards a set of mutually agreed targets that we'll monitor as we go. Are you happy with that?"

They were all smiling. Leon said "Ralph, you are a true businessman and I would be happy to accept your terms. Do we have a deal?"

I stood up and shook his hand, then Paul's and Martin's. Leon said "Welcome to the Millikan leadership team, Ralph. I am looking forward to getting this WIP project finished off and getting our other businesses into shape. The process for the new model will start to take shape over the next few months, so I think it might be a good idea for you to allocate one day per week to keeping the project team in good order while you are transforming the other businesses. Is that okay?"

"Sure Leon, that sounds just fine".

"Okay then, Ralph. I think you need to go and talk to Brian".

And with that, I gave them all a parting nod and a smile and I left to go and find Brian.

When I got to his office, Brian was talking to one of the supervisors so I waited until he was free and then I walked up to him and said "Howdy partner".

He looked at me sideways and said "What do you mean Ralph?"

I told him about the meeting with the directors and when I got to the part about him working with me to transform the other businesses he burst out laughing. He said "Ralph, I don't know what it is about you, but the most fantastic things happen to you, and I could not be happier. I would love to join you on this project. I think the next two years are going to be amazing". He stood up and shook my hand. Seems like I had a new partner and I also could not be happier.

I told Brian that we could discuss the detail of how we would work together but for now the priority had to be the WIP project. I set off to touch base with everyone in the team to make sure that they were all doing the right thing in their area. They were all working outside of their comfort zones and I knew they would need lots of support. That was my job, and I was going to do it well.

I spent a lot of time in the Final Assembly area, our pilot programme for the rest of the business. If we got that part right then we had a template we could use everywhere else.

Mal was doing his best impression of an air traffic controller when I arrived there. He was handing work out to the temporary team and looking just about as busy as I had ever seen him. When he saw me he said "Hello Ralph, how can I help?"

I replied "Mal, I was just about to ask you the same thing. How is it going down here?"

Mal said "It is going really well. I am having to spoon-feed most of the new guys but I know the work content in here very well, so I can do that okay. Robert is keeping the parts coming at the right time. I have had a good look at the plan and I think that our realistic finishing point to get through the bulk of the WIP in here is going to be 3 weeks from today, roughly one week ahead of schedule".

"Is there anything else you need?"

He stroked his chin for a moment and said "I think we need to record what I am doing in here so that we can do the same in the other departments. There is no sense in reinventing the wheel".

I nodded and said "I agree with that, Mal. Let's get together at the end of the day and we can discuss it with the rest of the team".

Mal agreed, and I set off to go round the other departments to see all of the other team members.

Around 4:30 we all reconvened in my office to compare notes.

I let Mal go first, as he was running the pilot programme in Final Assembly and he gave us a good rundown on what he was doing to get the team fully trained and how he was managing the process. He had basically made a list of the work content of every car in priority sequence. He had then shown a small team how to do job number one and told them do that job on every car that had the parts available. Then he had done the same for job number two and then three until he had allocated every job to the temporary crew. Because he had them working on one specific task they had picked it up very quickly and were soon doing it as well as the normal full-time guys on the line. It was a simple approach that clearly worked well.

We then had a long discussion within the team about how we could use this methodology in the other areas. Some were saying that they could do it just the same and others were saying that they could not do it at all because the process was so different.

At a natural break in the discussion I said "Okay who thinks that they can use Mal's methods in their area?" Three hands went up. I said "Okay, that is great. You guys can start to do that tomorrow. Just work closely with Mal to get the details right and we can start when you are ready. Those of you that cannot use these methods, I will come round to see you in your areas tomorrow morning and we'll work out together how to move forward. Are you all okay with that?" I got the right number of nods and smiles and we decided to call it a day.

When I was driving home I sent a text to Maricel. It had 3 short words in it. I love you.

By the time I had reached home she had texted me back. I love you too.

I sent her another, saying "Come on home, baby. I have some fantastic news".

Ten seconds later I got another message "Come and get me!"

So I turned the car around and drove to her mother's house. It was so great to see her again. I hugged her so tight and we just stood there for a full minute before I took her to the car to take her back to our house. I shouted hello and thank you to her mother, and then we were on our way.

When we got back home, she sat on the sofa and I went to sit beside her. I told her all that had happened during the day and at the end of it she was just as blown away as I was. Then she said "So this is the start of your new adventure as a transformation consultant. It looks like we will not have to worry about money again for a long time. That means so much to me, Ralph. The thought of bringing a new baby into a home that was in turmoil, with no stable income, was just too much for me to bear. I'm sorry took off like that but I received four bills in the post and I just blew a fuse. I had no idea that you'd got your first pay check and I had no idea that all of this wonderful stuff was just around the corner. Anyway, I am a lot happier now but my body still feels like it is fighting me, so you'll have to make allowances for a little while yet".

I looked at her with a new and deeper understanding. We were going to be good from now on.

Walking the Walk

I started the next day by going to the areas where the guys were struggling to get the hang of it. I had begun to realise that this part of the 7 Steps to Profit was really important. I had experienced this in my previous life as well. Most managers can figure out what needs to be done, but it is not the 'what' that is the hard part. The hard part is to figure out the 'how', and most managers never get that far; and even if they do, they usually give it a casual glance and delegate it to someone else. I decided that I would never do that. I would spend whatever time was necessary with the people involved to work out the 'how'.

There is no black magic in this process. You simply get the right people round the table, set out the desired future state, and brainstorm ideas until the 'how' starts to emerge. When you feel it moving in the right direction you start to ask sensible questions to keep it on track, relevant and manageable. The trick is to always keep it as simple as possible, like Mal had done in the Final Assembly area.

At the end of the day we had worked out the 'how' for all of the other areas and the guys were happy that they could work with it going forward.

For now we had to keep track of what was happening in the Final Assembly area, so we decided to have a briefing session every day with Mal giving us all a full rundown on progress. By the end of the week we were ahead of our own schedule and Martin Kirkbride was delighted with the boost to the cash flow.

I IS FOR IMPLEMENT AND TEST
RALPH'S REFLECTIONS

This week had been another fantastic learning experience for me. I had learnt that running a pilot program is a mini-version of the real work to be done and is a safer and smaller environment to minimise the risk and to gauge how well the real thing will work when it is rolled out. If the pilot goes well it can be used to create a template for the rest of the business.

It's important to select an area of the business that will give you a springboard to success, and if you manage to create the right environment and the results can be spectacular. It is useful to make notes as you go and to improve things on the fly. You can learn something every day and from the unlikeliest places.

To give yourself the best chance of success, you should choose an experienced team to run the pilot and give them an experienced manager. You should keep it running to a plan and a priority sequence so that you can track it easily.

It is important to publish the results accurately as you go – do not dress it up. If it is going well, accelerate the program and get the results quicker; but you also need to be prepared for the emphasis and direction to change. If a change in direction does occur, then you should approach it positively. I now knew that the problem you actually fix is quite often not the problem you started out with.

Personal Life

This week had been the craziest of my life to date. On the work front I had been on a particular track and I thought that the team were doing really great. That was derailed in the space of five minutes and we were suddenly working on a much smaller project. I could have chosen at that point to get all bent out of shape, but I remembered what Sam had taught me and stayed positive and rallied the troops. As a result of that, I received the offer of my dreams and now my life was on a trajectory that I would never have dreamed possible. I have never believed in fate until now; but it seems like fate has smiled on me, and I consider myself to be very fortunate.

On top of all of that, Maricel and I briefly drifted apart and then got back together, and we are now looking forward to the birth of our new baby. Does it get any better than this?

I have a new business partner in Brian, someone I admire immensely, and I am sure that when he learns the 7 Steps to Profit as I have learned it he will be a superstar. He has natural people skills that I openly admit were lacking in my own personality only a few weeks ago.

I have not had a drink for weeks and I have not missed it one bit. I have started eating healthily and doing a very short daily exercise routine which I copied from Leon, and I am also turning into the green smoothie man! I have transformed my working life, my personal life, and my most treasured relationship all in an amazingly short time. I had Sam to thank for all of it, but true to the nature of the man, he would not take any credit for it. I hope that I can do such great work and inspire as many people as he has done in his life.

My journey has been short but meteoric and I am looking forward to a wonderful career ahead.

> To get the free in-depth video tutorial on this step of
> 7 Steps to Profit go to **www.90daystoprofit.co.uk/bonus**

7 STEPS TO PROFIT

6 Tracking
5 Implement & Test
4 Fine Tune
3 Opportunities
2 Review
1 Problems

CHAPTER SIX

T IS FOR TRACKING
SAM'S SESSION 6

I got to the session on Saturday morning after another brilliant yet strange week at Millikan. We had cleared out around 35% of the Final Assembly area WIP already and generated millions in additional revenue for the business. We were all feeling pretty good about the way things were going, and so were the directors. It still felt to me like I was only doing half a job but I was remaining positive as I remembered the words that Sam had told me a few weeks ago: these things happen in assignments all the time, so I had just decided to go with the flow for now. They had made me a fantastic offer, I had a new business partner, and my wife was back at home with me so life was looking very positive for the first time in ages.

Sam was in fine form and got us all kicked off by asking each of us to give an update on progress, and he asked me to go first. I was expecting to go last like I normally did, but I think Sam was keeping me on my toes.

I told the guys what we had done for the last week at Millikan and how we had made such a massive impact on the business by freeing up the cash from the surplus WIP and how we were now going to pause for reflection before we went on to create a completely new process for the new model launch. It was a pretty spectacular update, if I say so myself, and I was basking in the glory when Sam brought us back to reality.

"Great update Ralph. I am sure the business is doing really well and the directors are very pleased with what has happened so far. However, the biggest challenge lies ahead of you. Designing a new process inside an existing business is one of the toughest things you will do as a transformation consultant. There is so much to unravel before you can move forward. You also have to maintain current output whilst changing everything about the way that the new product is produced. Oh and by the way, you have to keep everyone safe and keep quality to a very high standard. So no pressure Ralph!"

Sam was right. I was getting ahead of myself as usual. The job was never over, as the improvement journey is one that does not have any end and indulging in self-congratulations at this point was a little premature to say the least.

I listened to the other guys giving their updates, but in my mind I was thinking about my new role at Millikan.

Sam called us all back to order and said "Okay guys, let's get on to step 6. So far you have identified what it is you are going to fix, you have gathered and analysed the available data, you have generated some options or Silver Bullets, you have selected an option to run with, and you have run the pilot program in a part of the business that will give you the best chance of success. You have come a very long way in a very short time. So what is step 6?"

Some of the guys were getting really good at this now and Tony, one the young guys, said "You have to measure what impact the pilot program has had on the metrics and decide if you should roll it out across the whole business".

Sam was clearly delighted, he said "Tony, that is exactly right. I would just add that it is not only the metrics that are in play at this point. You have to look at how the pilot program has affected safety, quality, cost, delivery, morale, and the culture in the business. You have to ensure that what you are going to rollout is not only going to get the right results, but that it is going to fit into all other parts of the business and be accepted universally by the people who will be using the new process".

We sat there for a few moments letting that statement sink in when Tony asked the question that we were all thinking: "So how do we do that?"

"Come on fellas, do you want me to spoon feed you?" Sam smiled.

He continued "I want you to think about this for 15 minutes, and when you have done that we can discuss what your thoughts are".

This was very clever because we had already learned about this technique earlier and now Sam was making us use it in earnest to get to a self-learning point that would help us all to consolidate and assimilate this lesson very quickly.

Sam left the room and we all started to think quietly to ourselves. My own preferred method was to sit very comfortably and clearly articulate the problem to myself in my own mind before starting to think about any possible solutions. The process of clearly defining the problem was very useful to me. It was almost as if the clearer you could make the definition, the more obvious was the solution.

As I thought about how we could achieve universal acceptance of the changes, it came to me that it was a continuation of the methods we had already used up to this point. We had to involve everyone in the area where the pilot was being run in the monitoring of the results. We had to be honest with ourselves and the staff, with nothing dressed up or hidden away. If there were any issues to resolve, we had to listen to them sincerely and address them quickly as we were going along so that the staff could see that we were not only listening but acting on their input. This way we could get a greater understanding and a sense of belonging in the project. Treat people with respect, include them in the process, and be honest and sincere. Sounded like a good recipe for success to me.

Just then Sam came back into the room and he could see I was deep in thought, which was probably why he asked me to give my version of events to the team. So I mentally gave my head a shake and I replayed exactly what I had been thinking moments earlier to the rest of the guys. This started a great discussion on human nature and interaction which went on for a few minutes before Sam called us to order. He said "Guys, you are all coming along really well. What Ralph has just said about the monitoring process and how to gain acceptance is exactly what I would have done in that circumstance, and I can tell from the discussion that you have all just had that there is some real brain power being applied to this. I am really pleased with your progress.

Now let me give you some more detail on how to do it".

In the SAS, once a mission is underway it's very common for the people taking part to give updates on progress at regular times and checkpoints along the way. This way the commanding officers can gauge how well things are going and can make corrections as the mission is moving forward. They can use their skills and experience to advise and guide the team on how to get the best results in the field based on the information that is being fed back to them. They can also give orders and keep people focused when their resolve is faltering.

For the next hour or so, Sam gave us the subtle hints and tips that he always provided in these sessions. It was clear that he was a very seasoned consultant and he had learned his craft fully and in great detail. He also had the gift of being able to get that knowledge into our heads very quickly. The gist of this session was to involve the staff in the design of new ways of working, so that it became their process and they felt a sense of belonging and ownership and also a commitment to make it work.

As we were packing up, Sam came over and asked quietly "How did it go with Maricel this week?"

"Well, I took your advice and went after her like I should have done in the first place. We got back together in the middle of the week and we are starting to build our bridges and to move things in the right direction. I am taking it slowly because I do not want to mess it up again, and she seems to be enjoying my company again. I am pleased with progress".

Sam looked at me kind of sideways and said "Business transformation is a great profession and I love it. It is also a metaphor for real life and you can solve virtually any problem, whether business or personal, using these techniques. You just have to use your imagination and adapt it to fit the situation. Whether it's your own personal development or your relationships, you can get a better result by applying this formula. I am sure you have twigged that by now, but I just want to make sure you're not missing any opportunities. I know that you will make a success of this, Ralph. You have already shown your intellect and your resolve at Millikan, and I am sure that you can do the same with Maricel. She will be in your life for much longer than Millikan will ever be, so make sure you get it right".

I looked at Sam with a new found sense of admiration. It was not easy for a tough guy like Sam to have this kind of conversation, but he had the skill to do it and do it well. I knew I had a long way to go but his confidence in me meant a lot and I promised myself that I would be successful in business and in my marriage.

I then told Sam about the offer that Leon Musket had made to me. He was absolutely delighted for me, and it showed. He said "When we have finished the last session we should all go out and celebrate. Me and my wife, you and Maricel, and Brian and his wife. It will be a wonderful celebration. What do you say Ralph?"

"I'd love to, Sam. I'll speak to Maricel and to Brian and we'll work out the details shortly. Thank you Sam, that is a very nice gesture".

"My pleasure, Ralph, you are probably the best student I've ever had. It is the least I can do".

I said "But I cannot forget that you were the one that introduced me to Millikan. This could and should have been your opportunity".

Sam looked at me patiently and said "Ralph, I have had dozens of those opportunities over the years and there will be plenty more".

He patted me on the shoulder and walked over to his Porsche. He waved as he drove off. I could not believe how lucky I was.

Tracking the Results

The next week at Millikan was a great week. I worked out the details of my next three assignments and Brian and I signed up to the new deal with Leon. It was one of the best weeks of my life. But I am getting ahead of myself again.

I often did my 15 minute of thinking time before most people were in the office and that's how I started the day with a clear head. Once I was clear on today's focus I went straight in to see Brian. I asked him to gather the team so that we could agree next steps for the week. Fifteen minutes later they were all gathered in my office and I got the meeting kicked off. I said "Okay Mal, can you give us a brief on what you managed to get done last week and the methods you used to do it?"

Mal spent the next 10 minutes giving us a blow-by-blow account of the last week. In a nutshell, he had gathered all of the temporary crew at the start of the week and had assigned them all to a single task per vehicle. Then he and three other trusted supervisors had trained them all in that single task. Because it was a single task they all learned their work very easily and quickly. They all started out quite slowly but they learned to speed up their tasks within a couple of hours. Quality was first class and the work was done to the correct standards. When they had finished their task on the first vehicle they moved to the next one on the sequence. The sequence of planned work in priority order was provided by Robert Cullen and each vehicle started with its original ID but it was assigned to another ID when the new parts were all fitted. Robert kept a running record of what the vehicles actually were when they came out of Final Assembly. When each person had finished their task they went to a tally chart and ticked off their vehicle number.

The whole thing was simple and effective. As they moved through the backlog, the finished vehicles were taken into the final testing area and prepared for delivery. Before they were shipped, the accounts department contacted the customer to arrange for bank transfer of the cash to make the final payment. Once confirmation of this payment was received, the vehicle was shipped to the agreed destination and another happy customer was taking possession of their Millikan super car.

In one week they had released close to £50m worth of vehicles from the WIP. It was a staggering feat and the directors were understandably delighted with this breakthrough. And to top it off, the cash was already in the bank.

We then spent a half hour discussing how these methods could be applied to all other areas of the business. The three guys who had already agreed to use similar methods in their areas were happy that they could do this, and we just had to work out the details with the local area teams. I then told them that they could go and engage with those teams and Brian and I would come around during the course of the day and work with them to figure out the 'How'. They all took off to their respective areas. There were three left, including Sarah and Brian, and I sat down with them to work out how we could possibly do something similar in their areas. It was clear that due to the nature of the work it was not going to be the same as Final Assembly, so we looked at the actual process in each area and came up with a possible approach for each one. We then asked them all to go back to the area and work with the team leaders and other key staff to agree on how it could be done. We told them that there was plenty of time to get this done as we were making such great progress in Final Assembly.

The key part was to pass on to all areas exactly what had been achieved in week one of the WIP reduction project. We agreed a simple message to go on to every notice board, and Sarah volunteered to go and put them all in place.

Brian and I then divided up the workload between us and set off to support the teams. I went to Final Assembly first, to see for myself how they were doing the work and recording their progress. I took photographs of everything they were doing so that I could use them when I talked to the other teams.

In each of the other areas I sat with the key people to understand their part of the process and what we could do to remove the WIP in their area. I also worked out with them how we could manage the WIP in a structured way once it had all been removed. In some areas there were buffers that had to be put in place and I did some calculations with the experienced people in those areas to work out what size those buffers needed to be and how they would work. We did this by simulating various types of work flows and looking at how the numbers changed as the work flows changed. What this revealed was that there was a range for the size of the buffers, and as long as you stayed within that range you could accommodate almost every situation, including breakdowns of key pieces of equipment for up to 8 hours. This was excellent learning for me and I was storing all of this knowledge to use in my next assignments.

At the end of that day we had been to every area and worked out what steps we would need to take in order to continue with the WIP reduction project in each one. Because of a company wide email from Leon everyone in the business knew about the success of the work in Final Assembly and they were all super keen to be part of the success story themselves.

The next morning I went to see Leon to give him an update. I tapped on the door frame and popped my head in. Leon was doing pushups on the floor and said: "Come on it! Only 3 minutes to go". He looked at me and smiled broadly, then motioned with his head for me to sit at his meeting table. I sat down and looked at my notes.

He carried on with his routine for a few more minutes then jumped up and said: "How are you doing?"

"Just great, Leon. I thought that I would give you a quick update and get your steer on where we should be going next".

"Fire away".

For the next few minutes I told him about the work that we had done in Final Assembly, the results that the team had generated, and the methods that we had used to get those results. He took it all in and blinked in his owl-like way which still disconcerted me even though I was getting to know him pretty well by now. He said "Ralph, this is excellent progress. Please pass on my sincere thanks to the whole team for the hard work they have put in to get this done".

"Thanks Leon I will do that. We were thinking that we would work backwards through the process, clearing out the WIP as we go. We would work with Robert and the planners to get a level of control and accountability into what we are doing, and also to put in place some means to manage the WIP once it is cleared. Robert has done some excellent work in this regard and I can tell you that he is a top class planner".

Leon smiled again and said "Thanks for that Ralph. I like Robert and I agree he is a great planner. I think that he can help you and the guys a lot to get this project finished. I think your idea of working backwards makes sense as it will work on the highest concentrations of WIP in descending order so we will get the biggest bang for our buck as we go".

He picked up concepts extremely quickly, so I was not surprised at his grasp of the situation.

He then said to me "Ralph, you have achieved so much in such a short time here and I can see a change in you personally as well. You have lost weight, you have a bounce in your step, and you look absolutely on top of your game. I think that your new choice of career has made you into a new man. You and I are going to have some fun in the next couple of years".

"Thanks for that, Leon. You're right. When I first came here I was not exactly filled with confidence. I had been out of work for a few months, my marriage was not doing that well, I was overweight, drinking more than was good for me. Since I have been trained by Sam and I have learned so much here I am definitely not the same person I was a couple of months ago. I have applied Sam's teaching to my personal life and my professional life and it is working a treat. I have also learned from you and the great people you have in your team, so this has been a very positive experience for me. By the way, thanks for referring to me as the guy who saved the business!"

He laughed at that and said "I meant every word, Ralph. Let me know if there is anything you need from me".

With that I got up, shook his hand and set off back for my office.

For the rest of that week Brian and I moved our way backwards from Final Assembly through the rest of the process. We took Robert with us to work out how to manage the numbers and the ID of each vehicle. Robert was a godsend and it taught me that a skilled and experienced planner could add tremendous value in a transformation process like this. I would never underestimate the value of a planner ever again. At the end of the week we had made even more progress in Final Assembly and we were ready to move forward in the other areas.

To cap off a fantastic week, Maricel and I had an unusual date tonight. I was going to take her to a yoga class for expectant mothers, followed by a meal at a fabulous vegetarian restaurant next to the river walk in the best part of town. We both felt like it was a new beginning for us. Maricel had gotten over her sickness and had started to blossom. She was more beautiful even than the day I met her. I had also learned how to communicate with her again. Now that the money worries were out of the way and she was not working, we could actually spend quality time together just enjoying each other's company. I had learned so much in this last couple of months and I was determined to use it all in a positive way going forward. My career and my personal life were now going to be managed well.

Have you ever had a day when you look back at where you have been and then looked forward to where you are going and realised just how lucky you are? That was one of those days for me.

T IS FOR TRACKING:
RALPH'S REFLECTIONS

This had been an unbelievable week for me. I had signed the deal of a lifetime with Leon and we had made fantastic progress with the WIP reduction project. The team was working like a well-oiled machine and things could not be better. I took some time out to jot down my thoughts and reflections:

It was clear to me that this part of the process was an open and honest appraisal of how well the Pilot Program was working. If it worked well, as in our case, then it was a pretty painless process; but I could imagine scenarios where it would not be so smooth, and I could see that it was a critical part of the overall success of the process. We had changed things around as we looked at other parts of the process that did not fit this exact model. The principles were the same throughout the process but you had to be prepared to put in the work to make it successful.

Simple recording methods, like the tally charts we had used, were perfectly good for what we had to do and there was no need for fancy spread sheets or computer-generated forms. It could all be done simply and quickly and it was best if it was done by hand. The key to this part of the formula was the willingness to take decisive action.

I had also learned that the communication aspect of this step was just as important as anything else and once the staff in other areas could see how successful we had been they wanted to be part of the success. It was infectious and that was a very good feeling. Once the makeshift recording methods had achieved the objective we could go back and systematise them later if we had to. Also, collaboration with local team leaders and operators in each department was key to making it work.

Local knowledge, plus their skills and expertise, were invaluable.

Personal Life

It felt great knowing that we had a financial future that I could depend on for two years or more and that the baby would be born into a safe and loving home environment. Maricel and I were getting along well and doing personal change together, which made it easier and more fun at the same time. Adding little habits to my day had made a massive improvement over time and I was now so used to doing them that they were on autopilot. I was happy, healthy, and loving life – a huge change from where I was just a few weeks earlier!

> To get the free in-depth video tutorial on this step of
> 7 Steps to Profit go to **www.90daystoprofit.co.uk/bonus**

7 STEPS TO PROFIT

7 Shape & Rollout
6 Tracking
5 Implement & Test
4 Fine Tune
3 Opportunities
2 Review
1 Problems

CHAPTER SEVEN

S IS FOR SHAPE & ROLLOUT
SAM'S SESSION 7

This was my last session with Sam and I was feeling kind of sad and kind of elated at the same time. We had just finished another great week at Millikan and we were really making excellent progress – and it was all down to the learning I had been lucky enough to get from Sam. He was the real reason that I had been successful, by teaching me how to create a business transformation using the 7 Steps to Profit, and I considered myself to be very fortunate. Last week I had paid the additional £5000 in full and I was not regretting it one bit.

I arrived a little early as usual and Sam was setting up at the front of the room. I walked over and shook his hand. He smiled at me and said "This is our last formal session Ralph, but I am sure we will remain good friends in the future. All of my students are special to me but you have surpassed all of my expectations on so many levels and you will be hard act for any future students to follow. You have been a pleasure to train, and I genuinely wish you well in your future career as a major league business transformation professional".

I was feeling a little emotional myself and I said "Sam, the pleasure has been all mine. You believed in me when lots of other people in my life thought that I was turning into a deadbeat and I thank you for that. My success is all down to the quality of your training and the way that you gave me such huge self-belief. I would really like to keep in touch with you and maybe we could even work together in future? Whatever happens I will never forget this time in my life. It has been awesome!"

"Thank you, Ralph. That means a lot to me. Now the others are starting to arrive so let's get on with the session".

I looked around and the room was starting to fill up so I went to my usual seat and we got started. Sam was in fine form as usual, and he said "Okay guys, let's make our last session one to remember. Who has got the best update for us this week?"

They all turned and looked at me as though they fully expected me to put up my hand but instead I said "Not this week guys, it is time for one of you to shine".

So one of the other guys started to tell us about his week and the others quickly followed. The updates were all good, and it was clear that these guys were becoming experts at business transformation. Before it was my turn, Sam said "Okay guys, that's a good summary. Now tell me: what is step 7?"

They were all ready for this one and several hands shot in the air wanting to be first to answer. Sam picked a young guy called Rory who said "This is the step where it all comes together. Everything we have done so far has been leading up to this moment. Now we make the adjustments from our monitoring process and roll it out across the business with confidence".

I thought that his answer was probably the best of the whole course, and Sam was delighted. He laughed and said "Rory, I could not have put it better myself. At least some of my teaching must have rubbed off on you!"

We all laughed and I could tell this was going to be a really good session.

Sam went through the details of how to rollout the 7 Steps to Profit to all parts of the business. There were lots of things to remember about this step and I was making tonnes of notes, but I also found myself drifting off into daydreams as I could see how the whole process fitted together and how it all made so much sense.

Sam taught us that we should rollout the program across the whole business after we have communicated the success of the pilot program, including any changes we had to make as we went along. It was very important to be clear and transparent to all concerned. It was also important to get input from all other parts of the business about how to do the rollout. Where should it start, how should it be done, and by whom? How do we link the results to the metrics and Key Performance Indicators of the business? How do we make it stick? And so many more things – by the end of the session we all had our heads full of new ideas that we could not wait to go an implement.

Sam then said "Okay guys you have heard me making military analogies for the last six weeks, so how would you describe this step in military terms?"

I thought about this and said "Is this the part where you use the knowledge and the advantage you have gained by running a successful mission to go on and win the war?"

Sam was beaming. He said "Exactly right, Ralph. In business, the quest for success is a never ending journey and in the military it feels just the same. There is always another threat, another battle to win, another enemy to fend off. I have used my military training to fine tune my consultancy skills, and the two are very similar. The military taught me to act and behave in a logical and disciplined way; and business transformation fits right into that mindset".

All too soon the session was over. Sam called us to order and said "Guys, as you all know, this is our last session. I think you will all agree that it has been a blast. I can sincerely say that you have been a total pleasure for me to teach and I hope that you all go on to be very successful business transformation professionals. You all have done such a great job and you all deserve it".

We all stood and applauded. Sam was a little taken aback at this and waved us back down into our seats. He said "Thank you all for being such great students. Now go out into the world and make it a better place".

We applauded again and then young Tony got up and walked over to Sam. He was holding a bag in his hand and he said to Sam "On behalf of the whole group, I would like to give you a little token of our gratitude", and he handed the bag to Sam.

Sam looked a little embarrassed but he took it in good part and said "Do you want me to open this now?"

We all cheered and shouted yes.

He opened the bag and took out a cube, about six inches on each side. Inside the box was another smaller box, then another smaller box, until he finally opened the seventh and last box and it contained a silver key ring with a finely carved silver bullet attached to a solid silver chain. Sam took it out and looked at it for a few moments. Then he noticed that the bullet was inscribed. He read it out: "Thank you Sam. We will always remember the wisdom you have taught us. Class of April 2017". He looked a little sheepish once again and said "This is the most thoughtful gift I have ever received, so thank you guys. Now get out of here before I start bawling!"

We all laughed and started to move out. We shook hands with Sam before we left and there was a tremendous feelgood factor in the air. Sam followed me out and said "Ralph I know that you will be successful in business – you've already demonstrated how well you have taken to this kind of work. How are things in other parts of your life?"

I looked at him and said "Life is good, Sam. Thanks to your advice and encouragement!"

Sam put his arm around my shoulder and said "I knew you could do it, Ralph. Good luck with your career and make sure you keep in touch".

And that was the end of my final session with Sam. I felt a strange sense of loss at that moment, but it soon passed, and I headed off home.

Shape and Rollout

When I got to work on Monday morning I dropped my bag into my office and went in to see Brian and Mal. They were both at Brian's desk and looking in good spirits.

I asked Brian if we could get the team together after the morning meeting to agree what we were going to do this week. Mal said "Should I attend Ralph? I know what is happening down in Final Assembly and all the guys have their work for the day".

I said "Sure Mal, you can help us get the logic right and set us off on the last leg of the WIP reduction project".

An hour later we were all assembled in my office around the meeting table.

I called them to order and said "We are on the home straight of the WIP reduction project and the pilot programme has gone really well, thanks in large part to the work done by Mal and his team in Final Assembly". I nodded at Mal, who nodded back. I continued "So now we are at a crossroads, and we need to decide what the road map looks like going forward. I have had a brief word with Leon and he agrees that the most sensible way to do this is to work backwards through the process so that we work on the highest concentrations of WIP in descending order. The question for this team is do we agree that is the right thing to do?"

Robert Cullen was smiling and he said "Normally Ralph I would agree with that suggestion, but I have been giving this a lot of thought over the last few days and I actually have to disagree".

He had me intrigued, so I said "Okay Robert, you have been the brains behind the pilot programme, so I will bow to your greater experience in these matters. What do you have in mind?"

He got up and went to the flip chart and drew the process in block diagram form like I had done when I first arrived at Millikan.

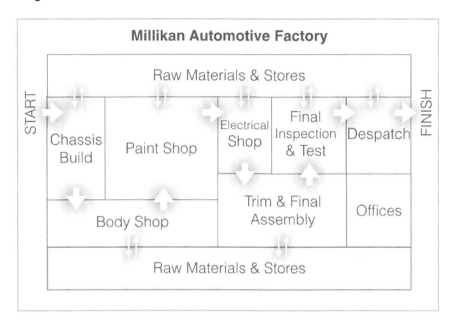

He said "In the Electrical Shop, each vehicle is fitted with a set of wires and cables that we call a loom. To get the best results in this area, we need to go to one-loom-fits-all solution. If we don't do that, we will have to revisit that area quite quickly because the WIP will start to accumulate without that technical solution in place".

Brian and Mal were both nodding and Mal said "I have been thinking about that, and I think that there is a quick way to get there. We already have one station which takes all of the part-finished looms and adds in the optional extras for each vehicle. We could modify that bench very quickly to be a fully comprehensive loom building station, as all of the options are already known at this point. Once that one station is modified I can get a team of electricians to build another eleven just like it, and that will give us enough work stations and build capacity to keep in front of Final Assembly at all times on a single shift".

I was impressed with the maturity that Robert and Mal were both showing at this point. It was like the team had started to drive itself.

I agreed that they both had good points and said "So now what do we do?"

Robert took the lead again and said "We have WIP left in three main areas, if we exclude buffers for the time being. Those areas are Body Shop, Rework and Final Paint, and the Electrical Shop. I suggest that we start with the Rework and Final Paint area, as that is where we can make the biggest impact in the shortest time. We can train a team, similar to what we have done in Final Assembly, and clear out the cars sitting in that area pretty quickly. It will push work into the other areas, so we may need to offer some overtime to take up the slack. I reckon it will take two weeks to get that area cleared out and I am hoping that will be enough time for the new loom-building stations to be built. If that's the case I would then propose to move into the Electrical Shop and use the single looms to finish off the WIP vehicles in there. That will take another two weeks. Then we go back to the Body Shop and figure out how to do that. The skills are very different in that area, so we will probably need to do something in collaboration with the Chassis Build area. This will all work if we manage the WIP in a tightly-controlled way at each part of the process. I have already got the planners working on that control mechanism".

At this point Sarah jumped in and said "That sounds like a good plan to me, Robert. I was working with the guys in the Body Shop last week and that is sort of where we were heading with our conversation. If we adjust the flow of chassis to match the workload of both areas we can create a team of skilled guys to focus on the WIP reduction, and the training will be far less because the skills are complementary".

This team just kept on getting better. I was proud of the way that Sarah had come on in this last few weeks. When I had told her about Brian and I moving on to other things she had asked me if I could get her on to the team for the other transformations, and I was thinking about how to do that. She would make a great Transformation Consultant with the right kind of coaching and training, and Brian and I were probably best placed to do that.

When she had finished speaking I stood up next to the flip chart and said "So let me play back what I just heard. The first area we should go after is the Rework and Final Paint, followed by the Electrical Shop – providing we have the loom building stations all built and operational at that point. Then we move back into the Body Shop and work out a joint effort with the Chassis Build area. Is that the road map that we are looking at?"

They were nodding so I said "Okay, then we need to run this past Leon. I think it would also be a great opportunity for Leon to give the whole workforce another update. What do you think guys?"

They were all smiling and Brian said "I think that another staff communication would go down very well at this point. We have done a pretty good job of letting people know what is going on, but Leon's sessions always go down well, so this is the perfect time for him to bring everyone up to speed. I will sort it out with Laura if you want to do the slides?" I was fine with that.

Then I got them all set up for the day. I said "I think we know what we are all doing. If you head back to the areas where you were last week, you can start to think about the detailed body of work that we will do in each area now that we have our road map". With that, they all left the office and headed to their allotted areas.

I walked up to Leon's office and stuck my head in the door. It was still pretty early and Leon was doing his seven-minute exercise routine. He looked at me with absolutely no embarrassment whatsoever and said "30 seconds left Ralph, come on in".

He finished his Hindu squats, picked up a small hand towel from the back of one of the chairs and wiped his brow and the back of his neck. He sat down opposite me at the table and said "I normally do this at home before my shower but I had an early conference call this morning so I thought I would do my routine in here. Everyone knows I do it, so it's not a big deal for me. I can't go a day without doing something physical and this seven-minute routine is perfect".

I said "I have been doing your routine for a few weeks myself, Leon, and I can tell you that it is working for me as well. I have lost weight and I am fitter than I have been in years. I might be imagining it but it also seems to be making me more alert as well".

Leon was smiling and he said "Good for you, Ralph. I think it does allow you to think better, as the blood flow is charged with oxygen and gets pumping quicker, so the brain must get some benefit as well. That's what I believe, anyway! Are you still on the green smoothies?"

"Yes, I am. I must admit they took a bit of getting used to, but now I am having one every morning and it feels great".

This was amazing. I felt like I was hanging out with my buddy Leon.

Suddenly the CEO appeared as if by magic. He said "So what have you got for me Ralph?" and blinked at me in that owlish way of his.

I told him about the team meeting that we had just had and the outcome in terms of the road map. I then asked him about the doing another comms session and he looked thoughtful for a moment. Then he said "I think it is a good idea to bring all the staff up-to-date with what has been going on, so let's get it scheduled. I am happy to do some of the session, and I would like you and Brian to do a joint presentation with me. You guys deserve a lot of credit for getting us to this point and raising your profile will be good for you and good for the business".

I was about to protest when he said "Great, so that is all settled. Let me know when it is arranged and we can go over the details. Anything else Ralph?"

"There is one other thing" I said, and I told him my thoughts about Sarah joining myself and Brian as part of the improvement team in the other businesses. He agreed straight away and said "That sounds like a great idea. I can see how much she has come on in such a short time. I don't want to lose her from the staff so how about we second her to your team for a couple of years, give her a working away from home allowance equal to her current salary, and pay her expenses. How does that sound Ralph?"

I said it sounded great and that I would discuss it with Sarah and come back to him. It kind of felt like he was expecting the question and had already prepared an answer for it ahead of time.

He smiled at me and I left his office feeling like I had been ambushed.

I found Brian in his office talking to one of the supervisors and I waited until he had finished and then told him about my conversation with Leon. Brian was happy to take part in the presentation and he said "That sounds good to me Ralph. Leon is an astute guy. He knows that it will be a good message to the whole workforce if we give a joint presentation. It will show visible proof of solidarity and it will position the whole thing where it needs to be".

There was Brian the ace communicator coming to the fore. I was going to enjoy learning from him.

The basics of the presentation were quite simple. We were giving everyone an update on the WIP reduction project with numbers where appropriate. The methods used were explained in a bit more detail and there was an explanation regarding the decision to hold back on the process redesign until the new model launch. Then we were explaining the road map to complete the WIP reduction project and what it would mean in each area, before asking for their support.

When I had it drafted I sent it to Brian and Leon for comment. Within a couple of hours we had it knocked into shape and we were ready to go. Brian and Laura had set up the area where we did the previous comms session. Brian sent out a note to all the supervisors asking them to gather everyone together the next day at the same times as the previous session. It never ceased to amaze me how such a large company could move so quickly. But that was a reflection of Leon's style. He never hesitated about anything, he was always so sure of himself, and this trait was evident in most of his key staff as well. I was pretty sure I would not find this in all other companies.

Next morning Brian and I got to the comms area a little early to set up the laptop and projector and Sarah came over to join us. She said "I am really going to miss doing all of this good stuff with you guys. I hope that I get the chance to do it again in the future".

I said "Well, Brian and I have already spoken about this, and I managed to have a quick word with Leon about it yesterday. He has asked me to make you an offer to join us".

She beamed her dazzling smile at us both and said "I accept!"

I was bowled over by this and I started to protest "But you haven't heard the offer!"

But she was not to be put off, and said "I don't care what the offer is. I want to do this kind of work with you guys so whatever Leon thinks is a fair offer is good enough for me".

So that was settled! Our team had grown by another one and Brian and I were both delighted.

Leon arrived just as the area was filling up and he said "Hi guys, I will open up with the first two slides then I am going to hand over to you two. I hope you have decided who is going to do the next bits. I will take over again for the last slide and the questions".

Brian and I had already decided which parts we were doing, so we both nodded our agreement. Then Leon brought the session to order and we were off and running. Leon was his usual polished self and he set the scene nicely. Then he handed over to me and I gave them all the details about the success of the pilot programme, including the massive boost in cash flow. Brian got up and described the road map in detail and handed back to Leon.

This was when it started to get interesting. Leon took charge and said

"These last two months have been some of the most eventful of my working life, and that is saying something for me". Everyone laughed because we were all well aware of the incredible things that Leon had done in his life. He continued "Ralph came into the business and put together a fantastic team of people who have achieved some wonderful results. I have already described Ralph as the guy who saved our business and I am not exaggerating when I say that. His contribution has been remarkable and I thank him personally for that. I also said to him when he arrived that if he worked some magic and turned the business around that I would give him a car. Today I would like to make good on that promise. Bring out the car".

I was astonished. The crowd parted and a brand new silver Millikan cruised silently up to the podium. The driver got out and handed me the electronic key fob. I was in shock.

Leon carried on as the applause died down "Ralph is a very modest guy and I am sure he is having a bit of trouble taking this all in. This particular car is a bit special. Every car is signed on the glove box by the guy in Final Assembly who is responsible for finishing the build. Well this one is signed by some guy called Leon Musket, so it might be worth a bit more than the average Millikan. I have one other piece of news in the same vein. When we took him on, our banker Simon Brown said that he would consider a bonus for Ralph if he managed to turn around the business in 90 days. Well he has done it in much less than that and we would like to show our appreciation. So I'm happy to present Ralph with a stock option certificate with a face value of £100,000 at the current stock price. If he hangs on to it for a couple of years it could well be worth a lot more than that".

I stood there gawping at the certificate in Leon's outstretched hand and I timidly took it from him and looked at the number. It was real alright.

Leon was leading the applause and I could feel my face getting red. Leon motioned me to take the microphone and I took it off him. The applause died down and I said "Leon your generosity is boundless. I was not expecting any of this. All I can say is thank you from the bottom of my heart". And with that the applause started again. This was definitely not the comms session I was expecting!

I looked over at Brian and Sarah and I could tell that they had been part of the arrangements for all of this just by the smiles on their faces.

Leon brought us all back to order again and said "Well that concludes our comms session. I am sure it is one that Ralph will not forget in a hurry. Are there any questions?"

Some wag at the back shouted "Any more free cars, Leon?"

He was obviously expecting this because he jokingly shouted back "No, there's not – now get back to work you lot!"

And with that the crowd started to disperse. A number of them came up to me and shook my hand. It was the most surreal experience I have ever had.

Leon came over and shook my hand as well. He said "I always look after the people that look after me, Ralph, and you have done an exceptional job here. I know that the team helped out and I will work out a bonus for them as well – but the drive and the momentum came from you and that is something for which we are all grateful".

I said "You could have told me what you were going to do!"

He just smiled and blinked and said "That wouldn't have been anywhere near as much fun!" And he turned and headed back to his office.

The rest of the day passed in a blur. We got the rest of the comms sessions done without any further incident, although Leon made mention of the bonuses he had given me so that by the end of the day everyone in the business knew what had happened.

That night when I got home and told Maricel what had happened, she burst into tears. She said "It's only a few weeks since we could barely afford the electricity bill, and now we'll never have to worry about money again if we are sensible with our investments. I can hardly believe that this is happening to us".

I called Sam and told him what had happened, and he was delighted. He hinted that he had given Simon Brown a bit of a nudge to make some sort of gesture, but I think that even he was impressed by the size of the bonus that I had been given.

Whatever happened in my business transformation career from here onwards would never surpass this achievement. Of that I was sure, but Sam had told me that he gets these kind of offers and bonuses on a regular basis, so who knows?

S IS FOR SHAPE AND ROLLOUT: RALPH'S REFLECTIONS

This was the end of one process and the start of another. I could now use the learning from the pilot programme to define how to rollout the WIP reduction to the rest of the business. I also knew it was important, as in all the other steps, to communicate the true results to the whole business and not sugarcoat it.

In order to move forward confidently it's important to create a road map for the rollout process and gain buy-in from the team and from the areas where the work will be done.

It's equally key to measure progress on the rollout and also the impact on the Key Performance Indicators and the effect on the cultural aspects of the business.

You have to work with the team to understand the 'how'. Most managers never get this far. They get to the 'what' and then stop, leaving the team to figure out how to actually implement the changes. I would not make that mistake. In this regard, you have to use the skills and experience of the team members to get the best result, and at the same time you need to gain buy-in from the senior team and ask the rest of the business for their support.

Personal Life

I thought that I had been through a pretty amazing time last week, but this one was totally over the top. I had not really expected anything like this. Things had gone really well in the business and there was no doubt that a lot of people had contributed to this fantastic result, but they all seemed to be really pleased that I had been given such a public show of appreciation from Leon.

Maricel and I were getting along better than ever before and I had learned so much in these last two months about what not to do in a marriage. I was never going to be such a fool again when it came to safeguarding my relationship with her.

This had been a total transformation for Millikan and it had also been a total transformation for me and my relationships. I would never be the same person again and I had a future that seemed to be full of promise. I am so glad that I met Sam Newton in that gas station.

I had learned so much from Brian, from Robert Cullen, from Martin Kirkbride, and so many other great people at Millikan. There are super heroes in every business – they are just disguised as ordinary people with ordinary jobs. You just need to give them a challenge and they will appear.

Time for you to go and find your super heroes and start your own transformation.

> To get the free in-depth video tutorial on this step of
> 7 Steps to Profit go to **www.90daystoprofit.co.uk/bonus**

7 STEPS TO PROFIT

7 Shape & Rollout
6 Tracking
5 Implement & Test
4 Fine Tune
3 Opportunities
2 Review
1 Problems

CONCLUSION

You have now been through the complete 7 Steps to Profit from end-to-end. If you follow the process in this book and use it as a template you will transform any business in a very short time. If you use the graphics and grids as we have shown them in this book, you will be able to engage any workforce in this process and keep them up-to-date with what is happening as well.

We believe this book will be valuable to any business owner, senior manager or business professional that needs to transform a business quickly and efficiently. Of course, you need to have a number of skills to be able to do this at the highest level. You should be honest with yourself about your own skill level, and seek out training and coaching to allow you to become more proficient over time. As you practice this formula you will begin to understand how powerful it really is and also what skills you need to improve for you and your staff to become more expert at using this process across all parts of the business.

We are able to teach and train you and your key people in these critical skills, and this will give you even better results as you make progress using these tools.

If you would like to become part of the 7 Steps to Profit community or gain access to any of our business transformation products please visit us at www.90daystoprofit.co.uk and we will be happy to assist you in your path to true business excellence.

Good luck on your transformation journey.

BUSINESS TURNAROUND DICTIONARY

Terms used in this book and in business generally

Buffers = storage capacity between work stations or departments. Buffers are used in a process to regulate the flow of product through the business. There are often times when parts of the process break down. If you have part finished product in the buffers you can continue to run until the breakdown is fixed without losing overall output. They can also be used to cater for different levels of capacity between the stages of the process and even for different shift patterns between processes.

EBITDA = (Eebit-Dar) This is a financial term used to describe profitability of a business. It stands for Earnings Before Interest, Taxation, Depreciation and Amortisation. This is a key measure in the valuation of a business and can be expressed as a multiple. For example a business may be valued at 10 x EBITDA. So if a company has an EBITDA figure of £10m and the multiple for the industry is 10 then the business could be valued at £100m.

ERP = Enterprise Resource Planning - these are usually large and complex software packages which are used to integrate and manage every part of a business from sales prospecting through to manufacturing, supply chain, logistics, quality, HR and Finance. Some famous ones are SAP, Oracle, Baan, CGI, Deltek, Epicor, Pegasus, Sage, Technology One, Workday and many more.

FVE = In this setting FVE stands for Finished Vehicle Equivalent. Sometimes it may be expressed as FPE which is Finished Product Equivalent. It is used to describe the component parts of a major assembly. For example in the Millikan factory there are a number of departments and each department has a different way of measuring their output. The FVE measure allows the business to normalise the output back to a common denominator which in this case is finished vehicles.

Golden Rules = In business terms a Golden Rule is something that should always be in place no matter what. For example a Golden Rule of planning may be that you cannot plan to produce a product when you do not have enough raw materials to finish the product. If you ignore this rule it is possible that you could start to make a product and have to finish it part way through because you have run out of parts or materials.

Kaizen = Japanese term describing the process and practice of continuous improvement. Some people also use it to describe the creative problem solving process used in breakthrough events. Some reference sources describe it as "Change for the better" but in reality there is no direct English translation.

KPI = Key Performance Indicator - this is a high level business measure that is used to gauge performance in various parts of the process. For example Sales Order Intake may be such a measure. Other measures such as Overall Factory Output, Defect Rate, Net Profit could also be classed as KPI's.

OTIF = On Time In Full - relates to customer service performance. Customers will often measure suppliers on how many of their orders are delivered on time with every order line complete. As a pure measure it is very harsh. If a single tiny item is missed from a 1000 line order the true score on that order is zero. This is why a lot of businesses use softer measures such as DTP - Delivery to Promise or VLF - Volume Line Fill which are percentage completion measures.

PLC = Programmable Logic Controller - this is basically an industrial digital computer which has been designed and built to operate in harsh or challenging environments. They are used to control manufacturing processes, such as vehicle assembly plants, printing presses, paper converting lines, food manufacturing plants and many more. They may allow production and assembly processes to achieve high levels of reliability and repeatability and they are also easy to use in terms of programming and fault finding.

SOP = Standard Operating Procedure - the process or procedure for carrying out a specific task or production operation. They are used to train people to carry out the task that is being described. The best practice for these documents is to make them as visual as possible with very few words so that language issues are minimised. Sometimes these SOP's can be made into simple videos which can be scrolled over and over in the workplace so that repetition is used to embed the training quickly.

TAKT Time (Pulse) = the customer demand or product demand divided by the time available to produce. For example if your customer demand for widgets is 200 per day and your factory is working an 8 hour single shift pattern then your TAKT Time for each widget is 8 x 60 / 200 = 2.4 minutes on a single workstation.

Trigger Points = an event that creates another type of activity. For example a trigger point may be a certain stock level of component parts that requires a purchase order to be raised for replacement parts. This could be that when a bin of parts is empty a new purchase order is raised to buy another bin full of parts.

WHAT WE DO

One-On-One Coaching	Organizational Consulting	Team Trainings
Are you a consultant looking to sharpen your skills? Our one-on-one coaching is a must if you want to distinguish yourself as a results-driven expert.	Are you a business owner who needs to transform their business? Let us execute the 7 Steps to Profit for you, while you focus on what you do best.	Are you a senior manager with a struggling team? Our live, in-person Team Trainings help your team turn around faster than ever before.

Are you ready to transform your business today?

Schedule a free, 30-minute Discovery Call with our team of experts to jump start your business transformation.

Email us today at: **iwantprofits@90daystoprofit.co.uk**

"Steve was a revelation. The time taken to produce our mainstream products has reduced by approximately 40% with a consequent improvement in throughput and a reduction in WIP. So impressed were we with our improved performance that we have agreed a stage 3 improvement plan but only if we could have the continuing services of Steve Shoulder"

~ **Mike Kilroy** - Financial Director ELCB UK

Our Clients:

"Steve has been inspirational in the way that he has coached me and other members of the team in what has been a very difficult time for the business. Without his efforts we would have been an early victim of the recession"

~ **Tony Fawcett** - MD Kitchen Exchange UK

"Steve managed to take control of a seasonal and volatile business and turn it into a stable and productive environment. The performance improvements and cost savings he has achieved with his team have made a big difference to the profitability of the group in the last year. We will continue to use his methodology in the future"

~ **Peter Rush** - Group MD Hozelock International

FREE BONUS MATERIAL

This book is dedicated to the people who want to turn around their business and maximize their profits. To help you achieve this goal in 90 days or less, we have created the following FREE bonus material to the book:

1. 7 in depth step-by-step tutorials on 90 Days to Profit

2. PDF resources and frameworks to use in your business

3. Access to Live Webinar where you can get direct access to the experts

To get the free book guide and get started on maximizing your profit using our proven 7 Steps to Profit system, please visit:
www.90daystoprofit.co.uk/bonus/

ABOUT THE AUTHORS

Erlend Bakke is a Norwegian serial entrepreneur, #1 international bestselling author, popular podcast host, consultant, and speaker. He is a turnaround expert who helps companies go from loss to profits in 90 days or less. Having launched successful companies as a self-funded entrepreneur, he has an excellent grasp on what it takes to make businesses prosper in a competitive and challenging environments when resources are scarce. His success places him in the top 7% of all entrepreneurs in the world. He knows what it takes to grow and transform businesses quickly and profitably. Today, he spends most of his time between Oslo and London.

Steve Shoulder has grown businesses by up to 770% in one year using creative means to improve top line and bottom line growth. He is a business transformation expert with consistent international success in manufacturing, technology and service businesses. He has transformed dozens of underachieving companies by rebuilding their strategy, restructuring operations, increasing sales, raising output and productivity, reducing waste, improving product and process quality and positively impacting bottom line profitability. He is a subject matter expert in Lean Manufacturing methodologies and a consummate team builder at all levels in a business. His success is driven by leadership, growth and return on investment. He is able to galvanise and energise management teams and get them all facing the right way in pursuit of clearly articulated and agreed targets.

Connect with us:
www.90daystoprofit.co.uk/

Contact us:
iwantprofits@90daystoprofit.co.uk

THANK YOU FOR READING
90 DAYS TO PROFIT!

Profits are only 7 steps away…

7 STEPS TO PROFIT

7 Shape & Rollout

6 Tracking

5 Implement & Test

4 Fine Tune

3 Opportunities

2 Review

1 Problems

www.90daystoprofit.co.uk/

Made in the USA
San Bernardino, CA
16 March 2017